THE AMERICAN LGBTQ RIGHTS MOVEMENT

AN INTRODUCTION

KYLE MORGAN & MEG RODRIGUEZ

Humboldt State University Press

Humboldt State University Library
1 Harpst Street
Arcata, CA 95521-8299
hsupress@humboldt.edu

digitalcommons.humboldt.edu/hsu_press

Texual content is licensed under Creative Commons Attribution-ShareAlike 4.0 International (CC BY-SA 4.0)

Use of textual content outside the Creative Commons license agreement and Fair Use requires written permission from the author and an HSU Press representative.

Use of the photographs outside of Fair Use requires written permission from the respective copyright holder. Photograph attributions are located at the back of the book.

Interior and cover layout and design: Carolyn Delevich
Interior and cover layout: Kyle Morgan
Cover Image: Photograph by Pat Rocco, Pat Rocco Photographs and Papers, ONE Archives at the USC Libraries

ISBN: 978-1-947112-44-5

HSU PRESS IS DEDICATED TO IMPROVING THE HUMAN CONDITION AND OUR ENVIRONMENT BY SHARING KNOWLEDGE, CONNECTING COMMUNITIES, AND PROMOTING UNDERSTANDING OF SOCIAL, ECONOMIC, AND ENVIRONMENTAL ISSUES.

THE AMERICAN LGBTQ RIGHTS MOVEMENT

AN INTRODUCTION

KYLE MORGAN & MEG RODRIGUEZ

HUMBOLDT STATE UNIVERSITY PRESS

ACKNOWLEDGMENTS

THANK YOU to the Los Angeles LGBT Center, Los Angeles Unified School District, ONE National Gay and Lesbian Archives at the USC Libraries, and Project SPIN for making this project possible.

Thank you to Joseph Hawkins, Jamie Scot, Greg Williams, Tracy Moore, and everyone on the ONE Archives Foundation for putting faith in myself and Meg Rodriguez to conduct this project.

Thank you to the LGBTQ archives who contributed materials for this publication:
- ONE National Gay & Lesbian Archives at the USC Libraries
- GLBT Historical Society
- Kinsey Institute Library and Archives
- Gerber/Hart Library and Archives
- Library of Congress Archives
- New York Public Library Manuscripts and Archives Division

Thank you to all the individuals who shared their photography for this publication.

Thank you to Loni Shibuyama, Michael Oliveira, Bud Thomas, Pat Allen, David Moore, and Jeff Snapp from the National Gay & Lesbian Archives at the USC Libraries, and to Marjorie Bryer from the GLBT Historical Society for all your amazing support. I tear up just thinking about every one of you.

Thank you to Lillian Faderman, Chris Freeman, Joseph Hawkins, Loni Shibuyama, Michael Oliveira, Carolyn Weathers, and all the others who provide such vital feedback on the publication.

Thank you to Carolyn Delevich for your wonderful book design.

Thank you to everyone who shared their stories and made this book possible.

PUBLIC REVIEW

The American LGBTQ Rights Movement: An Introduction provides a detailed, well-organized, and visually compelling overview of a frequently overlooked historical subject. Indeed, the LGBTQ rights movement has become one of the most visible and powerful movements in recent American history, yet LGBTQ history as a topic is often ignored in our society's history curricula.

This book is geared towards readers who know little or nothing about this subject, especially college and high school students, as well as general readers with a curiosity about LGBTQ history or politics. It succinctly describes the oppressive social conditions under which LGBTQ people lived throughout the 20th century, then provides a superb primer on the key organizations and leaders that fought back against these conditions. It describes the earliest gay rights (or "homophile") organizations from the 1950s, the transition towards more radical 1970s-era "gay liberation," the bleak days of the AIDS crisis in the 1980s, resurgent activism in the 1990s, the rise of gay marriage, transgender visibility, and a host of other important issues.

Along the way, the book explores the broader diversity of the LGBTQ community, especially in terms of race and ethnicity, creating a collective portrait of the LGBTQ movement that reflects this diversity. The contributions of women are amply highlighted throughout the text.

The book is divided between a readable, detailed, concise historical chronology and individual biographies of key figures in the history of the LGBTQ movement. The book is richly illustrated with dozens of photos of political demonstrations, influential people, and LGBTQ social life throughout the 20th century. It includes a useful appendix with fascinating primary documents and suggestions for further reading and study. Readers will come away from this book with a deep understanding of where the LGBTQ movement has been, the challenges it has faced, and where it might be heading in the future.

Craig M. Loftin teaches in the American Studies Department at California State University, Fullerton. He is the author of *Masked Voices: Gay Men and Lesbians in Cold War America* and editor of *Letters to ONE: Gay and Lesbian Voices from the 1950s and 1960s*.

TABLE OF CONTENTS

1 THE BEGINNINGS — 1
- PSYCHIATRY — 8
- MILITARY — 9
- GOVERNMENT — 11
- CRIMINAL JUSTICE — 12
- MEDIA — 14
- LGBTQ COMMUNITY — 15

2 THE HOMOPHILE MOVEMENT — 18
- THE BEGINNINGS OF THE MODERN LGBTQ RIGHTS MOVEMENT — 25
- ACTIVISM GAINS MOMENTUM — 29
- IMPACT AND INFLUENCE — 32

3 GAY LIBERATION — 34
- GAY LIBERATION — 40
- POLITICS — 41
- DECRIMINALIZATION AND DISCRIMINATION — 45
- STUDENTS — 46
- PRESS — 47
- MEDICINE — 49

4 PRIDE IN DIVERSITY — 50
- RELIGIOUS, RACIAL, AND CULTURAL IDENTITIES — 58
- TRANSGENDER ACTIVISM — 60
- BISEXUAL VISIBILITY — 61
- LESBIAN-FEMINISM — 62

RESPONSE TO ADVERSITY	**64**
BACKLASH	66
NATIONAL LEVEL ACTIVISM	68
THE AIDS ERA	**70**
AIDS	77
BENEFITS AND FAMILY	84
MARCH ON WASHINGTON	85
BISEXUAL ACTIVISM	88
THE LGBTQ RIGHTS MOVEMENT	**90**
VIOLENCE AND HATE CRIMES	96
MILITARY SERVICE	98
DISCRIMINATION	99
MARRIAGE	100
TRANSGENDER EQUAL RIGHTS	109
BATTLEFRONTS	**112**
RELIGIOUS FREEDOM	114
TRANSGENDER EQUAL RIGHTS	114
VISIBILITY	116
APPENDICES	**118**
TEN ORGANIZATIONS TO KNOW	120
TEN TEXTS TO KNOW	123
TEN HISTORY BOOKS TO KNOW	127
TEN COURT CASES TO KNOW	130
GLOSSARY	132
PHOTO CREDITS	135
BIBLIOGRAPHY	139

THE BEGINNINGS

1900 – 1968

[PSYCHIATRY
MILITARY
GOVERNMENT
CRIMINAL JUSTICE
MEDIA
LGBT COMMUNITY]

The Beginnings

PERSONAL
STORY

> "[I am writing you] if only to tell someone where we are, and why we are here; even if only to have someone on the outside worry about us."

WHILE DARREN AND I were visiting West Chester [Pennsylvania], a group of hustlers stopped us and wouldn't let us pass. After taunting us, one of the kids **punched me** in the stomach and kicked me in the face, while Darren yelled for the police. Finally they left, and Darren and I ran to the train station, when we were picked up by the police and taken to headquarters. It seems the hustlers realized the seriousness of what they had done, and in an attempt to protect themselves they told the police that it was Darren and I who solicited them! And I, who was beaten and kicked, was accused of assault, for it was said that I placed my hand on the rear of one of them. I won't even mention **"police brutality"** because I know it would be censored. Darren and I are waiting in this prison; waiting, but we don't know what for. We have been in this prison nearly a month now, with at least 4 more to go until we have a trial—all this simply because we cannot afford bail or an attorney.

Naturally, we've lost our jobs, and while we're waiting, we're probably losing

The Beginnings

our house and furnishing—all because a bunch of college hustlers won't tell the truth!...As we may only write two letters a month, this is my second. My first plea for help went unheeded, as will, I am sure, any further letters I may write. My family never wants to see me again—there is no one Darren and I can turn to for help. [I am writing you] if only to tell someone where we are, and why we are here; even if only to have someone on the outside worry about us. But what we are really hoping for is help to fight this case—a **most profound injustice**... Now that you know that we are in prison for a crime that we did not commit, I can only beg that you will do anything possible to help us. Please sir,

– Richard

NOTE. This letter was written to *ONE Magazine* in 1964. The magazine editors located a lawyer for Darren and Richard, and the two were released from jail. Source: *Letters to ONE* by Craig Loftin.

DEFINITION OF TERMS

Although the terms gay, lesbian, transgender, and LGBTQ (lesbian, gay, bisexual, transgender, and queer) are used in this chapter, these are not terms people used in the early to mid-20th century. Homosexual was the term most often used for lesbian and gay in this era. Queer was considered a derogatory term, unlike the positive all-inclusive meaning it has today. No term existed in the English language for transgender prior to the 1950s. In the 1950s and 1960s, transsexual became the most widely used term.

The Beginnings

1920s Harlem offered black lesbians and bisexuals a relatively safe place to engage in same-sex partnerships. Artists were usually quiet about their gender preference, but others like Gertrude "Ma" Rainey (top) and Gladys Bentley (below) were more open to claiming a lesbian or bisexual identity.

LGBTQ REPRESENTATION dates back to the earliest human civilizations. However, gay and lesbian communities only started to gain visibility in America with the development of industrialized urban centers in the late 1800s, most notably in New York. In 1903, New York police, under pressure from religious morality groups, conducted the first known raid targeting gay men. The Armed Services launched its first known investigation of homosexual behavior in 1919, with a probe into the activities of its cadets in Newport, Rhode Island. Although the military had a long history of persecuting homosexual activity dating back to the Revolutionary War, the Armed Services only officially made consensual sodomy a criminal offense in 1920.

Alcohol prohibition from 1920 to 1933 saw a period of greater freedom for LGBTQ people. Illegal speakeasies allowed LGBTQ people relatively safe places to congregate away from police intervention. Performers such as Gene Malin, Ma Rainy, and Bessie Smith openly espoused gay and lesbian identities, while female impersonators such as Julian Eltinge became popular international performers. Books with gay, lesbian, and transgender themes such as Virginia Woolf's *Orlando* and Radclyffe Hall's *Well of Loneliness* garnered wide popularity. Annual drag-queen balls drew thousands of participants in New York, while smaller balls gained popularity across the nation.

PSYCHIATRY

THE PATHOLOGIZING OF GAY and lesbian people began with the invention of the term homosexual by mental health professionals in the late 1800s. As the profession of psychiatry grew in prominence, mental health doctors grew increasingly presumptuous they could identify and ultimately transform gay, lesbian, transgender, and intersex people into heteronormative adults. In 1952, the American Psychiatric Association (APA) officially codified homosexuality as a mental disorder in their Diagnostic and Statistical Manual (DSM). Although this listing has since been removed from the DSM, mental health experts of this era employed a number of unsuccessful therapies in an attempt to cure homosexuality in their patients.

Psychotherapy, popularized by Freud at the turn of the century, utilized psychoanalysis, hypnosis, group therapy, and other verbally-based techniques to attempt to cure gay, lesbian, and transgender people. Behavior modification therapy, an attempt to cure same-sex impulses by associating them with negative stimuli, gained popularity in the 1950s. Maximum-security mental health facilities, such as Atascadero State Hospital, allowed mental health professions to employ more extreme methods including electric shock, lobotomies, sterilization, and drugs such as succinylcholine (a drug that simulates the feeling of dying) to try to cure patients of their homosexuality.

The rising stature of the psychiatric profession, as evidenced by the establishment of a National Institute of Mental Health in 1946, had implications for LGBTQ people far beyond mental health

DR. HARRY BENJAMIN 1912 – 2002

DR. HARRY BENJAMIN WAS BORN IN BERLIN, Germany, in 1885. He moved to New York in the 1920s and started a practice focusing on endocrinology and gender identity. From then until the 1960s, he was the go-to person for transgender people seeking medical treatment in the United States. Dr. Benjamin assisted Christine Jorgensen, Reed Erickson, and Renée Richards, among others, to medically alter their physiology and to provide social and legal support. Benjamin, and a network of doctors and psychologists, established the Harry Benjamin Foundation in the 1960s to assist transgender people in obtaining surgery. In 1966, he published the groundbreaking *Transsexual Phenomenon*. Benjamin retired in the 1970s and was honored as a pioneer for his work. The influential Harry Benjamin International Gender Dysphoria Association (HBIGDA) was named in his honor.

The Beginnings

services. During World War II and thereafter, the military used psychiatric evaluations as the basis for discharging gay and lesbian service members. The Immigration and Nationality Act of 1952 denied entry in the country to those with "psychopathic inferiority," a psychiatric term that was explicitly intended to deny access to, and later deport, gay and lesbian people. The 1950s Lavender Scare (to be explored in the "Government" section later) was justified, in part, on psychiatric views of the mental instability of gay and lesbian people. Print media in the 1950s published psychiatric-based articles on the homosexual threat to gender norms and on how to prevent homosexuality in children. Even the Revised Standard Version of the Bible added the mental health term "homosexual" in 1946.

Behavior modification kits used in attempts to cure homosexuality were available for purchase, including a stationary electroshock device, wireless shocker, and a personal shocker.

MILITARY

THE TRANSITION FROM WORLD War I to World War II led to a change in Armed Forces policies from discharging those who had committed the act of sodomy, to discharging those with "homosexual proclivities" —regardless of whether any sexual act had been committed. Nonetheless, because of the dire need for soldiers during World War II, the Armed Services did not strictly enforce its policies, and great numbers of gay and lesbian people served with distinction in World War II.

After the war, the number of expulsions for homosexuality increased three-fold. The Armed Force expelled many gay and lesbian service members under a blue discharge. Blue discharges were not dishonorable, but did disqualify the veteran from receiving benefits and subjected them to discrimination when seeking future employment.

The Veterans Administration discontinued blue discharges in 1947, but replaced it with an undesirable discharge category that continued to be used against gay and lesbian service members. In 1949, the Department of Defense issued a statement that required the expulsion of all known homosexuals from service. While the Korean War and the need for military personnel led to a temporary drop in discharges, the end of the war saw the high number of expulsions for homosexuality resume.

Lesbian service members of the Women's Army Corps work on a plane at the Army Air Force Base Unit at Patterson Field in Ohio in 1944. These women could not publicly reveal their sexual orientation during their service.

The Beginnings

GOVERNMENT

THE ANTI-COMMUNIST FRENZY following World War II led to the Lavender Scare in which gay and lesbian people were targeted by the federal government. Anti-homosexual crusaders argued that gay and lesbian people's innate immorality and mental instability left them vulnerable to blackmail by Communist agents. No evidence corroborated this accusation, but gay and lesbian people had no political influence nor advocates to counter the hyperbolic claims against them. In 1953, President Eisenhower signed Executive Order 10450, banning lesbian and gay people from working for the federal government or any of its private contractors.

Consequently, the FBI launched a campaign to root out gay and lesbian people from federal employment. Thousands of gay and lesbian people were ultimately fired as security risks from federal employment in the 1950s and 1960s. The investigation also had a broader impact, as unknown numbers of LGBTQ people simply quit their federal jobs rather than face a possible FBI inquiry. Many state and municipal governments, as well as private employers, followed the federal lead to root out gay and lesbian employees. In some professional fields, this campaign effectively created blacklists of gay and lesbian people who could no longer find employment in their respective fields.

BAYARD RUSTIN
1912 – 1987

AN OPENLY GAY AFRICAN-AMERICAN QUAKER PACIFIST, Bayard Rustin was one of the most important and influential civil rights activists of the 20th century. He schooled Martin Luther King Jr. about Mahatma Gandhi's philosophy of nonviolence. With King, he formed the Southern Christian Leadership Council. In 1963, he conceived and then organized (in just eight weeks) the March on Washington, site of King's "I have a dream" speech. However, on the eve of the march, he was denounced on the Senate floor as a "Communist, draft dodger, and pervert." Eventually Rustin was forced out of the civil rights movement by internal politicking in which his homosexuality left him vulnerable. He continued to advocate a protest agenda informed by a belief that "economic inequality is the graveyard of democracy." Rustin was posthumously awarded the Presidential Medal of Freedom in 2013.

CRIMINAL JUSTICE

AT THE END OF PROHIBITION in 1933, state liquor authorities formed to regulate the dispersal of alcohol. These authorities used their power to revoke the licenses of bars that served gay and lesbian clientele. Police enforced the regulation by raiding and shutting down bars that served gay and lesbian people. Purposefully vague local morals, lewd conduct, and disorderly conduct statues permitted police to harass and arrest gay and lesbian patrons with impunity. Because bars were the primary public places where gay and lesbian people congregated, the raids created an atmosphere of fear that permeated the community.

Police canvassed and ran entrapment schemes at public areas frequented by gay men. Police selectively arrested gay, lesbian, and transgender people for such transgressions as wearing clothing of the opposite sex, behaving as someone of the opposite sex, or even holding hands with a member of the same sex. Those arrested were vulnerable to violence from police and, if jailed, from inmates. If their arrest became known, they faced the loss of their jobs, eviction from their homes, and social ostracization. Arrestees often had little choice but to quietly pay their fines, rather than contest their arrest in

PEARL M. HART 1890 – 1975

THE FIFTH DAUGHTER OF IMMIGRANTS, Pearl M. Hart left school at fourteen to earn a living. However, she soon returned and earned a law degree from the John Marshall Law School in Chicago in 1914. Hart was the first woman lawyer to practice criminal law in that city, where she became a champion for social justice. As a public defender, she successfully defended women unfairly accused of prostitution and gay men arrested on dubious morals charges. In the anti-communist hysteria of the 1950s, she defended naturalized citizens accused of subversive activities whom the federal government acted to deport.

Hart helped to found and served on boards of many social justice groups, including the National Lawyers Guild and Mattachine Midwest. She taught law at her alma mater and worked pro bono for causes close to her heart. She sympathized with the needs of the most vulnerable in society and actively fought for the rights of children. She lived with her same-sex partner for thirty years and died leaving a meager financial estate and a huge legacy.

court and have their sexual orientation publicly exposed in local newspapers.

LGBTQ people were particularly vulnerable to extortion and violence. Victimized LGBTQ people rarely filed charges out of fear of exposure or that they would be the ones arrested. Perpetrators of violence against gay, lesbian, and transgender people could even claim what become known as a "gay panic" or "trans panic" defenses which justified any violence, including murder, in the name of protecting oneself against a same-sex advance. California became the first state to ban the use of such a defense in 2006, and as of 2019, has been joined by six other states.

Fears of homosexuality led to gay purges in local communities and universities. In Boise, Idaho, fear of an underground homosexual ring led to the questioning of roughly 1,500 people, of which fifteen were sentenced to prison, including one for life. In Florida, a years-long state funded task force successfully removed scores of gay and lesbian educators from public schools. Universities across the country saw an escalation of the expulsion of gay and lesbian students and professors.

In 1924 Chicago, Henry Gerber launched the first known homosexual rights organization in America, The Society for Human Rights (SRH). Police arrested Gerber and shut down the organization a few months after its founding. The police confiscated and never returned papers associated with the SRH publication, *Friendship and Freedom*, as well as Gerber's typewriter.

MEDIA

IN 1927, THE STATE OF NEW YORK banned theater productions that promoted homosexual content. In the 1930s, the Hays Code forbid homosexual content in movies. Book and magazine publishers commonly refused to print positive portrayals of gay, lesbian, and transgender people for fear of legal prosecution.

In the 1950s, print media gave voice to the psychiatric view that homosexuality was a mental illness and a threat to male and female gender norms. Articles advised how to rear children to ensure they did not become homosexual. Tabloids printed conspiracy theories of a gay and lesbian underground targeting children and family values.

In the 1950s, cheap and sensationalized gay and lesbian fiction became abundantly available. Called "pulp fiction" for the cheap paper it was printed on, these works utilized tragic cautionary endings so as to avoid their confiscation by authorities for promoting homosexuality. Still, the stories were popular in the lesbian and gay community because they were among the few sources of mass media coverage of lesbian and gay people.

This *ONE Magazine* cover story tells a firsthand account of a United States veterans' hospital employee who was interrogated and fired from his job for being gay. The task force responsible for the investigation coerced him to turn over his gay and lesbian coworkers in the name of purifying the hospital.

The San Francisco beat writers addressed homosexuality and bisexuality in their literature and poetry and harbored openly gay and bisexual members, including William Burroughs and Allen Ginsberg. Allen Ginsberg's *Howl and Other Poems* and William Burroughs' *Naked Lunch* both successfully fought off obscenity charges brought, in part, because of homosexual content.

LGBTQ COMMUNITY

DURING WORLD WAR II, the large congregation of men and women in same-sex environments in the military, and in United States factories, meant gay and lesbian people could find each other in numbers never before possible. After the war, many gay and lesbian service members decided not to return home, but instead remained in large port cities with other gay and lesbian people. Despite persecution, gay and lesbian communities flourished in most major United States cities and a few vacation areas such as Cherry Grove on Fire Island in New York.

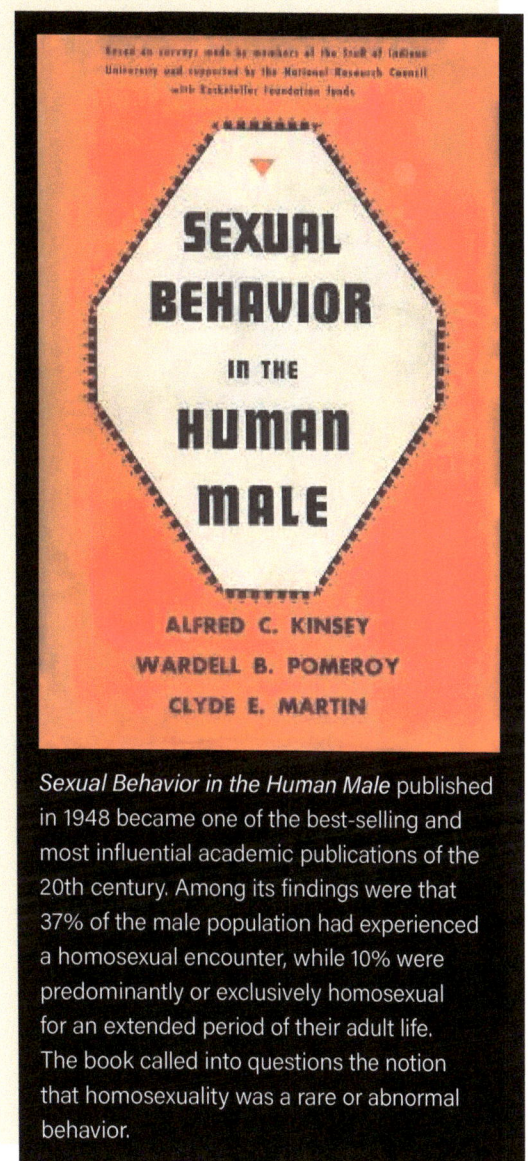

Sexual Behavior in the Human Male published in 1948 became one of the best-selling and most influential academic publications of the 20th century. Among its findings were that 37% of the male population had experienced a homosexual encounter, while 10% were predominantly or exclusively homosexual for an extended period of their adult life. The book called into questions the notion that homosexuality was a rare or abnormal behavior.

A few social-based groups emerged to meet community needs. One the first known incorporated LGBTQ groups in American history, the Veterans Benevolent Association, launched in 1945 as a social and support group for gay veterans. The interracial social club Knights of the Clock launched at the end of the decade. The Satyrs Motorcycle Club founded in 1954 in Los Angeles became one of the oldest continually operating gay organizations in North America and helped spawn the formation of gay motorcycle groups across the United States.

Other social gatherings were more informal. In-home parties provided protected spaces for LGBTQ communities. Reputed LGBTQ-friendly public parks and beaches, sports leagues, and even science fiction clubs provided other venues for same-sex people to meet and interact. *Swasarnt Ner's Gay Girl's Guide* in 1949 was one of the earliest to publish gay-friendly gathering places. Annual gay travel publications like the Damron guides and gay tours, such as those led by ONE Incorporated, emerged in the 1960s.

JAMES BALDWIN 1924 – 1987

JAMES BALDWIN SURVIVED AN ABUSIVE STEPFATHER, bullying, and poverty to become one of the great writers and civil rights advocates of the 20th century. He explored racism and the African-American community in his texts, including in the critically acclaimed novel *Go Tell It on the Mountain* and essay collection *Notes of a Native Son*. In his book *Giovanni's Room*, he dealt explicitly with a gay relationship, treating the gay characters as men first, rather than homosexual stereotypes. Baldwin himself was never in the closet and weathered enormous criticism for his sexual orientation. Baldwin spoke out against racism, homophobia, sexism, classism, and poverty all this life, a moral witness to prejudice and inhumanity in all its forms.

The Beginnings 17

Motorcycles, cars, sports, parks, and beaches each held social opportunities for same-sex interactions outside of the bar culture.

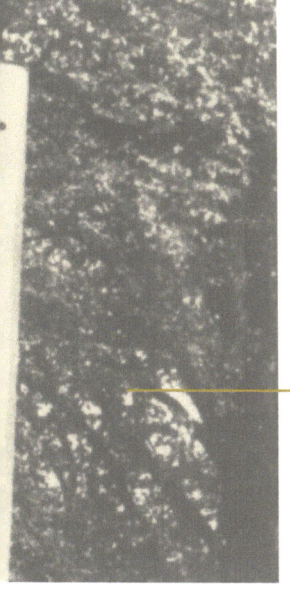

2

THE HOMOPHILE MOVEMENT

1951 – 1968

[
THE BEGINNINGS OF
THE MODERN LGBTQ
RIGHTS MOVEMENT

ACTIVISM GAINS
MOMENTUM

IMPACT AND INFLUENCE
]

PERSONAL STORY

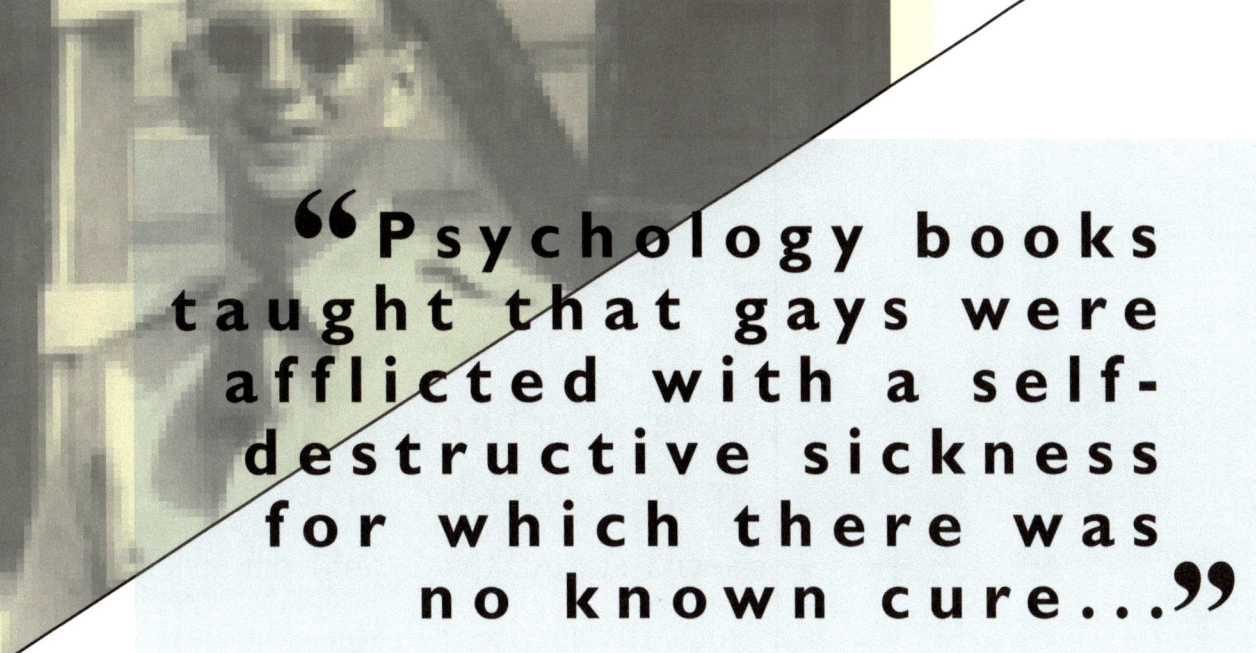

"**Psychology books taught that gays were afflicted with a self-destructive sickness for which there was no known cure...**"

THE GAY PERSECUTION and police raids of World War II and its Cold War aftermath were powerful warnings against "coming out" as gay or lesbian. There were almost no positive resources to help one figure out one's sexual orientation. I didn't know anyone who was gay. For most of us, it was **"go-it-alone."**

There was no relevant discussion in schools,

churches, or colleges. Psychology books taught that gays were afflicted with a self-destructive sickness for which there was no known cure, except perhaps psychotherapy designed to turn gays straight. This **mental disorder** carried with it a social stigma that would bar us from jobs. It was inconceivable that we could ever lead a "normal" life, much less settle down with a permanent same-sex partner. Many of us just forcibly shut down that side of our lives.

In college I enrolled in ROTC, whose stipends in the final two years I needed for tuition. I was acceptable enough to become a "Distinguished

The Homophile Movement

Military Graduate" with a lieutenant's commission in addition to my bachelor's degree, summa cum laude. I ranked fourth in my Officer's Basic course (out of 80), and served out my term in New York, undetected, with increasing responsibilities and top security clearance.

After I had landed a job teaching, one of my promising freshman students didn't return for a second semester. He had been arrested in a **police raid** on a gay bar. The police notified his parents and also the college's president, who had told him not to return to school.

– William Koelsch

DEFINITION OF TERMS

Although the terms gay, lesbian, transgender, and LGBTQ (lesbian, gay, bisexual, transgender, and queer) have been used throughout the text, these were not terms people predominantly used in 1950s and 1960s. Homosexual was the term most often used for lesbian and gay people in the era. Many gay and lesbian activists of the 1950s and 1960s preferred the term homophile to homosexual and referred to their fight for equal rights as the homophile movement. Queer was considered a derogatory term, unlike the positive all-inclusive meaning it has today. In the 1950s and 1960s, transsexual became the most widely used term for transgender. Today the term transsexual is used more as a subset of transgender if it is used at all.

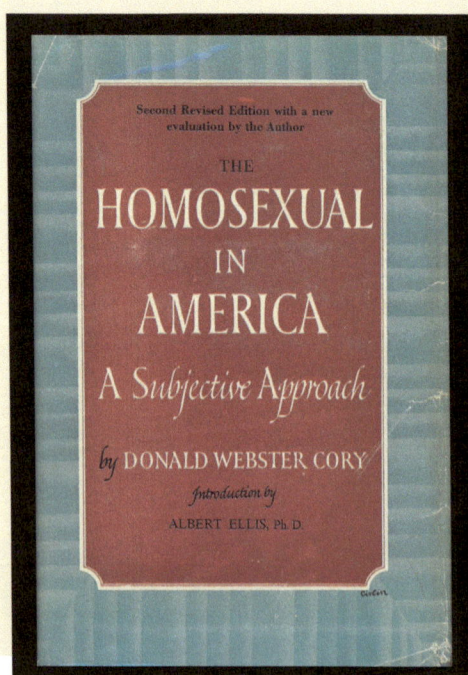

Donald Webster Cory's *The Homosexual in America: A Subjective Approach* published in 1950 was the first non-fiction book in the United States to identify gay and lesbian people as an oppressed minority group. Unlike most psychological accounts of the day, it criticized the idea that homosexuality could be cured and encouraged gay and lesbian people to shed their guilt and shame. The book's argument for the rights of homosexuals inspired activists of the era and set the stage for the gay rights movement to follow.

The Homophile Movement

THE BEGINNING OF THE MODERN LGBTQ RIGHTS MOVEMENT

THE POST WORLD WAR II ERA saw the formation of some of the nation's first LGBTQ organizations, including the Veterans' Benevolent Association in New York and Knights of the Clock in Los Angeles. Although these early organizations had no real impact on LGBTQ rights and mobilization. The first LGBTQ activist organization of note came together in 1951 when Harry Hay helped organize the Mattachine Society in Los Angeles. The Mattachine Society blamed an intolerant society, not gay and lesbian people, for the discrimination they faced. Hay argued that gay and lesbian people were a minority group oppressed by a prejudicial society, and they needed to organize to challenge their unjust persecution.

At first, membership in the organization grew slowly. Most gay and lesbian people feared they would be arrested or fired from their jobs if anyone knew they were a part of an LGBTQ organization. But

IN AN ERA THAT LABELED LGBT PEOPLE as mentally ill and legally criminal, Latino gay activist José Julio Sarria provided a public symbol of pride, determination, and revolt. Sarria's theatrical drag performances at the Black Cat bar in San Francisco were a popular theatrical attraction in the 1950s and 1960s. When he was arrested on a morals charge, he decided "to be the most notorious impersonator or homosexual or fairy or whatever you want to call me—and you would pay for it." His lyrics taunted the police who harassed him. He took to the streets in makeup and drag in an open challenge to local morals statues. He led the bar's patrons in renditions of "God Save Us Nelly Queens," enlisting them in the war against quiet shame and solitude.

Sarria ran for a city supervisor's seat in 1961, the first openly LGBTQ person to run for government office in the United States. Later as founder and head of the drag-based Imperial Court System, Sarria created an oasis for LGBTQ pride and celebration, as well as a fundraising force for LGBTQ rights causes across the United States. "You do good work, your work will fight your battles." Jose Sarria's work cast him as one of the most caring, devoted, and fearless leaders in the early fight for LGBTQ rights.

JOSÉ JULIO SARRIA

c. 1922 – 2013

Founders of the Mattachine Society include from left to right: Dale Jennings, Harry Hay, Rudi Gernreich, Stan Witt, Bob Hull, Chuck Rowland, and Paul Bernard. To avoid the local police and federal authorities, members met in secret at undisclosed locations and often did not know each other's full names.

in 1952, when the Mattachine Society successfully defended a police entrapment case against one of its members, excitement spread about the organization. Mattachine Society chapters formed across the United States and membership expanded rapidly. The success was short-lived. At the Mattachine Society's national convention in 1953, members forced Hay and the other original founders out because of their past communist ties. Although the following years saw membership dwindle and the national coalition crumble, local Mattachine Societies in Washington D.C., New York City, Chicago, San Francisco, Boston, and Detroit among others continued to work effectively for gay and lesbian rights into the 1970s.

HARRY HAY 1912 – 2002

HARRY HAY JOINED THE COMMUNIST PARTY in the 1930s, but soon grew weary of the party's anti-homosexual stance. In 1948, he proposed a group founded on the idea that homosexuals were an oppressed minority who must mobilize for civil rights. Two years later, Hay and four others founded the Mattachine Society.

Hay ended his marriage, resigned from the Communist Party, and dedicated himself to the Mattachine Society. Unfortunately, Hay's hope of leading a national movement ended when he and his fellow co-founders were ousted due to their past communist ties. After being called to testify before the House Un-American Activities Committee in Los Angeles in 1955, Hay retreated from public activism.

In the 1970s, Hay and his partner John Burnside became active in the gay and Native American civil rights movements. By the end of the decade, they had helped found the Radical Faeries, a tribal spiritual movement for building gay consciousness. Hay's reintroduction into LGBTQ activism revived interest in his past and early organizing efforts and led to his standing among many as the founder of the gay rights movement.

The Homophile Movement

(left to right) Don Slater, W. Dorr Legg, and Jim Kepner helped make ONE Incorporated a leading LGBTQ equal rights organization in the 1950s. Besides publishing *ONE Magazine*, the organization was the first to establish a public LGBTQ research library (1953), provide social services to the LGBTQ community (1953), host conferences on LGBTQ rights (1955), teach classes in LGBTQ studies (1956), and publish an LGBTQ scholarly journal (1958).

In 1953, a group of Mattachine Society members in Los Angeles came together to publish the LGBT periodical, *ONE Magazine*. Henry Gerber in 1924, and Lisa Ben in 1947, had each published short-lived gay and lesbian periodicals, but *ONE Magazine* was the first to sustain production and reach a national audience. *ONE Magazine* challenged the status quo with cover stories on same-sex marriage and federal anti-LGBTQ persecution. The magazine quickly drew the attention of the FBI and the United States Post Office. In 1953 and again in 1954, the local postmaster confiscated the magazine, claiming its positive portrayal of homosexuality violated federal obscenity laws. But in the 1958

CHRISTINE JORGENSEN
1926 – 1989

CHRISTINE JORGENSEN WAS NOT THE FIRST PERSON to have gender reassignment surgery, but she was certainly the most famous American to do so. A World War II veteran, George William Jorgensen always felt he was a woman trapped in a man's body. Because the United States had no facility for sex reassignment surgery, Jorgensen had the procedure in Denmark in 1951. Now known as Christine, Jorgensen became a media sensation upon her return to the United States in the early 1950s. In an era where the mainstream media did not discuss non-cisgender identity or sexual orientation, Jorgensen broke the silence by speaking to media outlets, touring as an entertainer and lecturer, writing a book, and having a movie made about her life. Her publicity raised the consciousness and visibility of transgender people to themselves and to the nation at large.

decision *ONE, Inc. v. Olesen*, the United States Supreme Court overturned the ruling, delivering the first Supreme Court decision in favor of LGBTQ rights.

In 1955 San Francisco, Del Martin and Phyllis Lyon helped found the Daughters of Bilitis, the first lesbian organization in the United States. Their publication, *The Ladder*, would be the only lesbian periodical in the United States over the next fourteen years. The Daughters of Bilitis expanded to several chapters across the United States and, in 1960, convened the first of a series of national lesbian conferences.

This 1959 autograph party for Harry Otis, author of *The Keval*, shows the interconnectedness of California-based gay and lesbian activists in the 1950s. This event included W. Dorr Legg of ONE Inc. (far left), Hal Call of the Mattachine Society (front with bow tie), gay-rights advocate Dr. Blanche Baker (in wheelchair), and Del Martin (right with white collar) and Phyllis Lyon (upper right) of the Daughters of Bilitis.

Phyllis Lyon
1924 – 2020

Del Martin
1921 – 2008

FOUNDING MEMBERS OF THE DAUGHTERS OF BILITIS, Phyllis Lyon (left) and Del Martin were as committed to activism as they were to each other. Aside from running the Daughters of Bilitis and its flagship publication, *The Ladder*, they were active in the Council on Religion and the Homosexual and helped launch the anti-police brutality Citizens Alert. They were the first lesbians to join the National Organization for Women as a couple, despite the anti-lesbian rhetoric prevalent at the time. Their book *Lesbian/Woman*, winner of the American Library Association's LGBT book of the year in 1972, was a formative text for the burgeoning lesbian rights movement. Later, Martin and Lyon developed into leading educators regarding domestic violence and human sexuality. Together for over fifty years, they were the first same-sex couple legally married in California.

The Homophile Movement

ACTIVISM GAINS MOMENTUM

IN SAN FRANCISCO IN 1962, gay bar owners and bartenders organized the Tavern Guild to combat police harassment of their bars and patrons. The Society for Individual Rights (SIR) formed two years later to push for broader LGBTQ rights. SIR combined social functions with political activities to become the largest LGBTQ organization in the United States. In 1966, it opened the nation's first LGBTQ community center.

A coalition of San Francisco gay and lesbian activists and religious leaders formed the Council on Religion and the Homosexual (CRH) in 1964. When police raided a CRH sponsored New Years Eve event in 1964, religious leaders stood side-by-side with gay and lesbian activists to condemn the police's targeting of LGBTQ people. The protest brought about a temporary halt to police raids on LGBTQ establishments and demonstrated the untapped power of coalition politics.

In Los Angeles, the first reported LGBTQ clash with police occurred in 1959 at Cooper's Donuts, where a mostly black and Latino LGBTQ clientele responded to the harassment of drag queen patrons by chasing officers from the establishment. Eight years later, PRIDE (Personal Rights in Defense and Education) led hundreds in protest when police raided the Black Cat bar in Los Angeles and brutally beat patrons and the bartender. The next year, bar owner Lee Glaze led a crowd of flower-carrying protesters into a Los Angeles police station to protest the arrests in his bar.

Black Cat Bar protest in the Silver Lake neighborhood of Los Angeles, 1967

In Washington, D.C. in 1961, Frank Kameny and Jack Nichols revived the Mattachine Society of Washington and fought to reform the federal government's anti-gay and lesbian policies. The group initiated a massive letter writing campaign aimed at federal staff and politicians, and in 1965, helped organize some of the first gay and lesbian pickets. They enlisted the help of the American Civil Liberties Union (ACLU), which had previously ignored LGBTQ discrimination claims. The Mattachine Society of Washington provided support to *Scott v. Macy* (1965) and later *Norton v. Macy* (1969), both successful legal challenges to the federal government's discriminatory policies.

In New York in the early 1960s, Randy Wicker, the one-man member of the Homosexual League of America, provoked mainstream newspapers and magazines to cover homosexuality and homosexual issues. Wicker, and members of the New York Mattachine and the League for Sexual Freedom, organized the first LGBTQ picket in 1964 when they protested military security lapses in regards to the confidentiality of gay and lesbian records. The New York Mattachine Society staged "sip-ins" the next year at New York City bars to protest the state's ban on serving alcohol to LGBTQ patrons.

In Philadelphia in 1965, the Janus Society, a homophile activist group founded in 1962, led a sit-in at Dewey's restaurant in response to a decision by the owner to refuse service to those in "nonconformist

FRANK KAMENY 1925 – 2011

IN THE 1950S, FRANK KAMENY WAS FIRED as an astronomer for the federal government when his homosexuality became known. Blacklisted from working in his profession, Kameny turned his frustration into political activism. Although he lost a four-year court battle for reinstatement as a government astronomer, he helped revive the Mattachine Society of Washington to agitate for reform of the federal government's discriminatory policies. He helped to organize some of the first gay and lesbian protests, enlisted the support of the American Civil Liberties Union for gay discrimination claims, and inspired LGBTQ activists with his fiery speeches and tireless activism.

Kameny's early battles with the federal government convinced him that the fight for gay and lesbian rights would be forever hindered until the American Psychiatric Association (APA) removed its listing of homosexuality as an illness. Although others had broached the issue, his inspiring speech before the New York Mattachine Society in 1964 ignited a heightened activism around the cause. Kameny remained actively involved in the issue for the next nine years, even speaking at the 1971 APA annual meeting, and helping end the APA listing in 1973.

clothing." In 1967, Charlie Brydon organized Seattle LGBTQ activists into ASK/US (Association for Social Knowledge of the United States), which later became the Dorian Society. This organization raised the visibility of the LGBTQ community in the Pacific Northwest and provided services to the community through its Dorian House. Bob Basker founded the Mattachine Midwest in 1964 in Chicago to combat a heightening of local harassment and discrimination against LGBTQ people. In 1966, the Mattachine Midwest led a picket at the *Chicago Tribune* and *Chicago Sun-Times* to protest the exclusion of LGBTQ news and advertising.

In 1963, Frank Kameny helped bring together the Janus Society in Philadelphia and Mattachine Society chapters in New York and Washington, D.C. to form East Coast Homophile Organizations (ECHO). In 1965, ECHO led small protests at the White House, Pentagon, State Department, and Civil Service Commission, and initiated the first in a series of Annual Reminder pickets outside of Independence Hall in Philadelphia. In 1966, gay and lesbian activist organizations came together in Kansas City, Missouri, for the first North American Conference of Homophile Organizations (NACHO). By 1967, the coalition claimed a membership of 6,000 individuals and organizations. By 1968, they had formalized a national campaign behind Kameny's "Gay is Good" slogan.

REED ERICKSON

1917 – 1992

REED ERICKSON WAS BORN RITA ALMA ERICKSON in El Paso, Texas. Independently wealthy, Erickson began his transgender transition under the care of sex realignment surgery pioneer Dr. Harry Benjamin in 1963 and changed his name to Reed. In 1964, Erickson founded the Erickson Educational Foundation, a charitable foundation primarily created to support research and services in transgenderism, gender identity, and sexual diversity. Throughout the 1960s and 1970s, Erickson supported conferences, publications, educational services, and media outreach on transgender topics. Erickson donated over two million dollars to various organizations including the Harry Benjamin Foundation, Johns Hopkins Gender Identity Clinic, National Transgender Counseling Unit, and ONE Incorporated. Through his generous philanthropy, Erickson advanced transgender medical and support services more than any individual or organization in the 1960s and 1970s.

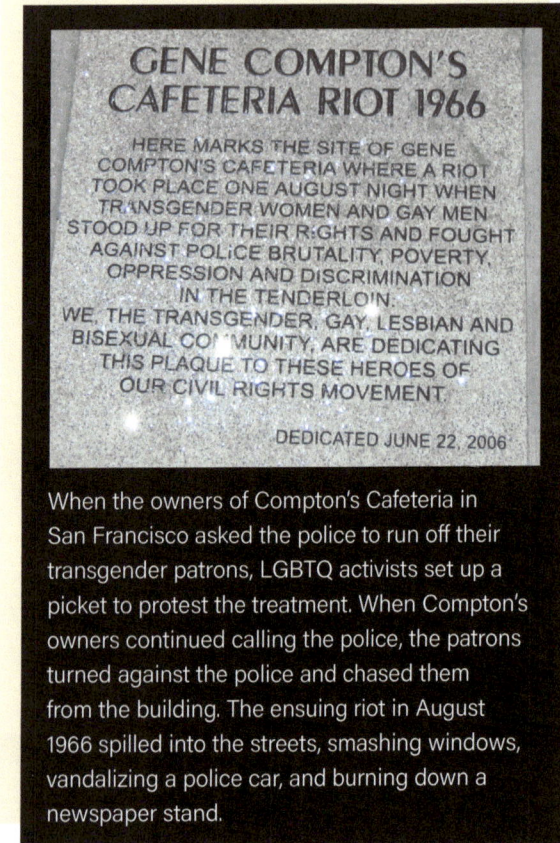

When the owners of Compton's Cafeteria in San Francisco asked the police to run off their transgender patrons, LGBTQ activists set up a picket to protest the treatment. When Compton's owners continued calling the police, the patrons turned against the police and chased them from the building. The ensuing riot in August 1966 spilled into the streets, smashing windows, vandalizing a police car, and burning down a newspaper stand.

IMPACT AND INFLUENCE

LGBTQ ACTIVISM of this era had limited impact on broader civil rights law. The Civil Rights Act of 1964 covered all Americans except those with disabilities, LGBTQ people, and undocumented immigrants. The Immigration and Nationality Act of 1965 removed a discriminatory quota system, but it strengthened the exclusion of gay and lesbian immigrants. By 1969, only Illinois had decriminalized sodomy (1961), while guilty sentences for sodomy in many jurisdictions could result in life in prison. LGBTQ people still suffered from vague charges relating to morals, lewd conduct, and disorderly contact that sent them to jails and mental institutions because of their sexual orientation or gender identity.

Regardless, this era saw a change in the mentality of the LGBTQ movement and set the stage for the successes to come. Before the 1950s, there were no activist-oriented LGBTQ organizations, no LGBTQ periodicals, and a worsening persecution of LGBTQ people. By the end of 1969, there were activist organizations throughout the American Northeast, Midwest, and West; open rebellion on the streets; and an increasingly visible and strident LGBTQ print media. Those courageous activists that came out of the closet to lead this charge risked their homes, jobs, families, and lives so that future generations would not be excluded from their civil rights.

The Homophile Movement

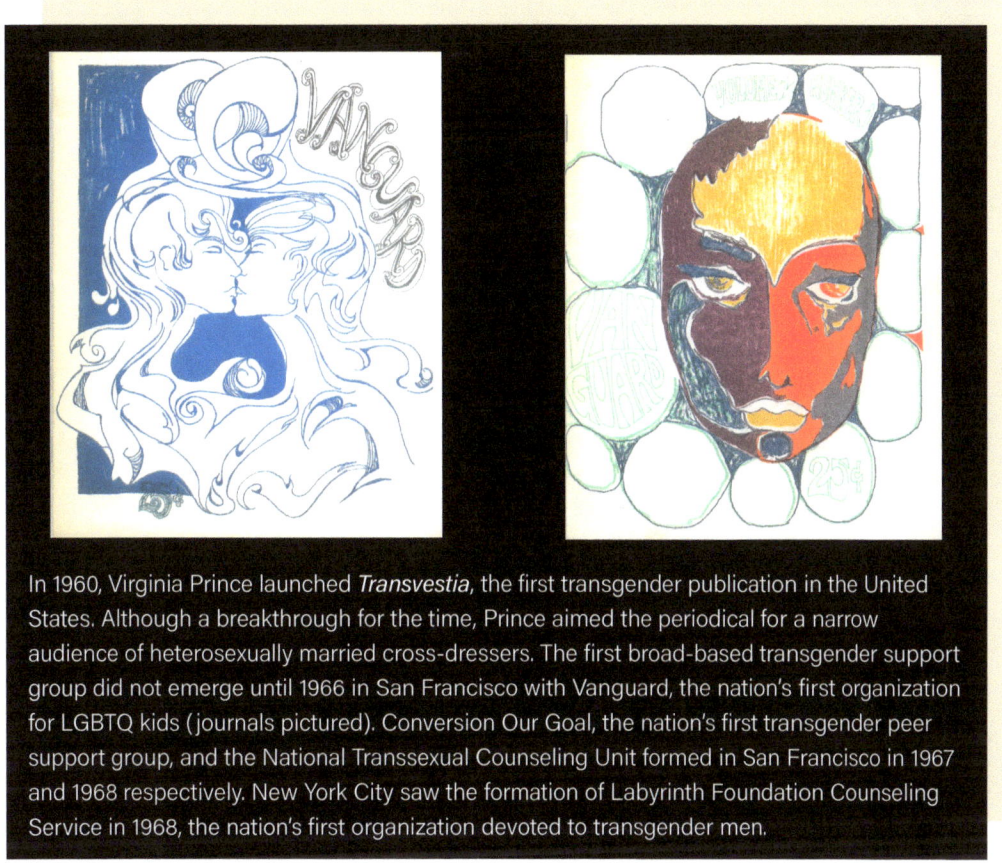

In 1960, Virginia Prince launched *Transvestia*, the first transgender publication in the United States. Although a breakthrough for the time, Prince aimed the periodical for a narrow audience of heterosexually married cross-dressers. The first broad-based transgender support group did not emerge until 1966 in San Francisco with Vanguard, the nation's first organization for LGBTQ kids (journals pictured). Conversion Our Goal, the nation's first transgender peer support group, and the National Transsexual Counseling Unit formed in San Francisco in 1967 and 1968 respectively. New York City saw the formation of Labyrinth Foundation Counseling Service in 1968, the nation's first organization devoted to transgender men.

Although the LGBTQ movement was inspired by the tactics of the Civil Rights and Women's movements, LGBTQ activists' involvement in the struggles of other civil rights causes was often fraught by homophobic biases. Bayard Rustin, a leading strategist of the black civil rights movement and organizer of the historic 1963 March on Washington, was pushed into the background when his homosexuality became public. Ivy Bottini, a founder and president of the New York chapter of the National Organization for Women in the late 1960s, was driven out of the organization amid a purge of lesbian members. Not until the 1970s would such biases soften as black leaders such as Huey Newton spoke out in support of LGBTQ rights and lesbian-feminism became an influential force in the women's movement.

3

1969 – 1980 GAY LIBERATION

[
GAY LIBERATION

POLITICS

DECRIMINALIZATION AND DISCRIMINATION

STUDENTS

PRESS

MEDICINE
]

PERSONAL STORY

Gay Liberation

> "They knew we were gay. We knew they knew it. They knew we knew they knew it. The game was on."

MAYBELLE AND BEE'S BAR was outside the San Antonio, Texas, city limits and harder to regulate for the police, sheriff, military police, and liquor control boards. Therefore, we could dance there. It's not that we were doing anything illegal. In 1963, we ourselves **were illegal**. If we got caught dancing with someone of the same sex, that would mean we were homosexual, and since it was against the law to be homosexual, we were subject to arrest.

Maybelle would leave the bar and come stand in the doorway between the bar in front and dance floor in back. If her red bandana was sticking out of her front pocket instead of tied around her neck, this was **The Sign**. Police coming. Police here. We would be dancing gayly, men with men and women with women, and in the time it took to say "Bossa Nova Cha-Cha- Twist," we switched partners in mid-beat, and seconds before the police appeared in the doorway, were dancing in male/female couples.

The police slowly circled the room, peering for a man touching another man's hand under the table, a woman's knee pressed against another woman's. They circled the room twice. They knew we were gay. We knew they knew it. They knew we knew they knew it. The game was on. When they caught someone being illegal, that is, being themselves, off that person went to jail. When they could catch a bunch of us dancing, they'd get a big catch for their paddy wagon. This time, we won the game, and they left grudgingly. They would be back. But for tonight, we turned the jukebox back on and commenced **dancing gayly**.

– Carolyn Weathers

GAY LIBERATION

DURING THE 1960S, POLICE departments across the nation enforced state bans on serving alcohol to LGBTQ people by raiding bars suspected of serving LGBTQ patrons. So when New York City police entered the LGBTQ-serving Stonewall Inn in the early hours of June 28, 1969, they expected the typical routine of shutting down the bar and arresting selected patrons. But when arrested patrons resisted and a threatening crowd gathered, police retreated back into the bar for protection. By the time that police reinforcements arrived, a riot had erupted in the streets that would continue for nights to follow. The moment would come to symbolize the beginning of the gay liberation movement.

The next year, commemorative marches and "gay-ins" were organized in San Francisco, New York, Chicago, and Los Angeles to coincide with the anniversary of the riot. New York's march, which started small with tens of people, grew to hundreds then to thousands as it entered Central Park. A Los Angeles contingent enlisted the help of the American Civil Liberties Union to acquire a city permit; it became the first LGBTQ march sanctioned by a city government. These marches developed into an annual event, grew in size and participation, and soon spread across the nation and the world in cities small and large as a reminder and celebration of the Stonewall Riots of 1969.

Jack Baker & 1942– Mike McConnell

IN 1970, MINNEAPOLIS RESIDENTS Jack Baker and Mike McConnell became the first national media celebrities of the LGBTQ rights movement when they held a press conference to announce their application for a marriage license. Not only were they denied the license, but the University of Minnesota withdrew McConnell's job offer. Baker and McConnell sued on both accounts. The Minnesota Supreme Court, in the first state ruling of its kind, denied Baker and McConnell the right to marry; and a federal appeals court upheld the University of Minnesota's right to deny McConnell a job due to his homosexuality.

POLITICS

THE MONTH AFTER THE 1969 Stonewall Riots, LGBTQ activists in New York City formed the Gay Liberation Front (GLF). The group capitalized on a newly energized community to introduce a radical activism into the gay rights movement. At its height, GLF had over 50 chapters across the United States, each initiating boycotts and protests against the discriminatory policies of local police, universities, businesses, and city governments. Although its unstructured organization and conflicting goals would quickly doom the group, GLF forever changed the LGBTQ movement. GLF members were responsible for launching gay pride marches, community service centers, and many of the era's leading LGBTQ activist organizations.

Reverend Troy Perry (in black) with partner Steve Jordan and Perry's mother (front seat) at the first gay pride parade in Los Angeles.

The Gay Activists Alliance, a splinter group from the GLF in New York, introduced "zaps," a non-violent, direct-action protest in which activists directly and publicly confronted politicians, celebrities, and businesses. These in-your-face protests forced their targets to address the issues of the LGBTQ community or risk continued public attacks. As more activist organizations adopted these increasing aggressive tactics, some elected officials and candidates for office at the local, state, and federal level began to publicly address the topic of gay and lesbian rights for the first time.

In San Francisco in 1971, Jim Foster founded the Alice B. Toklas Memorial Democratic Club, the first registered LGBTQ political club in the nation. Soon LGBTQ political organizations could be found in most major United States cities, forcing politicians to address the LGBTQ community in local, state, and national elections. In 1977, the Municipal Elections Committee of Los Angeles (MECLA) became the first openly LGBTQ political action committee in the nation. Although initially founded to influence city politics, MECLA's fundraising power expanded its influence into state and

Midge Costanza with glasses) arranged this first meeting of gay and lesbian leaders at the White House. Named the National Gay Task Force White House Conference, the meeting included Troy Perry (far left), Myra Riddel (third from right), Charlotte Spitzer (second from right), and George Raya (far right).

national politics. The organization quickly became the most powerful LGBTQ political group of its time.

With increasing political clout, gay and lesbian politicians and delegates began vying for political positions and offices. The 1972 Democratic Convention boasted the first openly gay and lesbian delegates. Two of the delegates, Jim Foster and Madeline Davis, spoke at the podium, the first LGBTQ people to do so at a major political function. By the 1980 Democratic Convention, the gay and lesbian contingent had grown to seventy-seven delegates. At that convention, the Democratic Party officially endorsed its first ever gay rights plank.

In 1974, Kathy Kozachenko became the first openly LGBTQ person elected to a government office when she won a seat on the Ann Arbor City Council in Michigan. Elaine Noble won a seat in the Massachusetts state legislature later

ELAINE NOBLE   1944 –

WHEN ELAINE NOBLE CAME OUT, her lover left her, she lost her job as an advertising executive, her tires were slashed, and she got obscene phone calls. So what did she do? She ran for a seat in the Massachusetts House of Representatives. Winning 59% of the vote, she was the first openly LGBTQ person elected to state office. Not only that, she was reelected two years later. In this photograph, she talks with future United States Congressman Barney Frank, who came out himself in 1987.

Gay Liberation

One gay, one lesbian, and one straight couple turned themselves in at the Los Angeles Police Department for transgressing the state's sodomy law. The police refused to arrest the activists.

1945 – 1987

MELVIN BOOZER

MELVIN BOOZER WAS A SOCIOLOGY PROFESSOR at the University of Maryland and president of Washington's Gay Activists Alliance. He was little known outside of Washington, D.C. when he approached the podium to deliver one of the most powerful speeches of the 1980 Democratic Convention. "Would you ask me how I dare to compare the civil rights struggle with the struggle for gay and lesbian rights? I can compare them and I do compare them, because I know what it means to be called a nigger and I know what it means to be called a faggot, and I understand the difference, in the marrow of my bones. And I can sum up that difference in one word: None."

Gay and lesbian delegates at the 1980 Democratic Convention.

in the year, becoming the first openly LGBTQ state representative. Minnesota State Senator Allan Spear came out as gay at the end of 1974 and then won his re-election bid in 1976, becoming the first openly gay man to be elected to government office.

In 1977, the National Gay Task Force (NGTF) collaborated with Midge Costanza, Assistant to the President for Public Liaison, on a meeting of gay and lesbian activist leaders at the White House. President Carter had not been informed of the meeting, and LGBTQ leaders would not meet with a sitting president until 1993. However, the event implied federal recognition of the gay rights movement and opened the door for future NGTF meetings with federal government agencies. By 1977, gay and lesbian activists had begun meeting with representatives of the American Civil Liberties Union and various women's rights groups to discuss common strategy. However, prejudice against LGBTQ people still trumped the promise of a broader collaboration; the Leadership Conference on Civil Rights rejected NGTF's application for membership.

IVY BOTTINI 1926 –

IN 1966, IVY BOTTINI BECAME A FOUNDING member of the National Organization for Women (NOW), and soon after, the New York chapter's second president. When she divorced her husband in 1968 and news of her being a lesbian became public knowledge, some NOW members spoke out against her, using the term "lavender menace" to describe the danger of lesbians in the women's movement. Bottini left NOW and relocated to Los Angeles, where she became a leader in the gay and lesbian rights movement. She helped lead the No on Briggs Proposition 6 campaign (the proposition intended to fire gay and lesbian educators from public schools), the Stonewall Democratic Club, and the Los Angeles Police Department's first Gay and Lesbian Police Task Force. She responded to the AIDS crisis of the 1980s by founding the Los Angeles AIDS Network and becoming a founding member of AIDS Project Los Angeles.

DECRIMINALIZATION & DISCRIMINATION

The demonstration against State Steamship Lines in 1969 was the first to protest employment discrimination in the private sector.

SODOMY LAWS HAVE BEEN active in the United States since colonial times and have been used to prosecute all types of non-procreative sexual activity. Although state sodomy laws often spell out no distinction between heterosexual and homosexual acts, in post-World War II America, the laws were disproportionately used to harass and arrest gay men. Because same-sex sexual activity was fundamentally not procreative, sodomy laws made presumptive criminals of all gay and lesbian people and justified the denial of their civil rights.

Illinois decriminalized sodomy in 1961. By 1975, only six more states had followed suit, and in 1976, the United States Supreme Court rebuffed a challenge to sodomy laws. However, the growing political clout of the gay rights movement forced increasingly rapid change in the second half of the decade. By 1979, twenty-one states had decriminalized sodomy, with another fourteen reducing the charge to a misdemeanor. By the end of the decade, 90% of the population lived under substantially decriminalized sodomy laws.

Although states resisted anti-discrimination legislation for LGBTQ people, activists at the local and federal level had more success. In 1972, San Francisco, East Lansing, and Ann Arbor, Michigan, enacted local anti-discrimination measures to protect gay and lesbian people in employment and housing. By 1977, more than forty cities and counties had implemented LGBTQ rights protections. In 1975, lawsuits such as *Norton v. Macy* forced the United States Civil Service Commission to drop its policy against the hiring of gay and lesbian people (except in the FBI and intelligence agencies). In 1980, the United States Office of Personnel Management banned discrimination against gay and lesbian people in all federal service jobs.

STUDENTS

THE STUDENT HOMOPHILE LEAGUE, under the leadership of Bob Martin, emerged at Columbia University in 1967 as the first officially-recognized LGBTQ student group. LGBTQ student groups gradually took root at New York University, Cornell, Stanford, and the University of Minnesota, but after the 1969 Stonewall riots, LGBTQ student groups spread more rapidly. By 1971, LGBTQ student groups had been recognized at sixty universities, while numerous others existed without official recognition.

LGBTQ student groups often had to overcome fierce opposition by university administrators for the right to be recognized. The Gay Students Organization (GSO), at the University of New Hampshire, scored the first victory in court in 1973 when judges ruled that the university could not deny the GSO rights that it provided to other student groups. Throughout the 1970s, LGBTQ student groups fought challenges to their funding, use of facilities, and university recognition. Not until state and United States Supreme Court rulings in the 1980s and 1990s would LGBTQ student groups overcome the last challenges to their constitutional rights of free speech and assembly.

BARBARA GITTINGS 1932 – 2007

"COMING OUT IN A PICKET LINE in 1965 was downright revolutionary. We were just at the start of cracking that cocoon of invisibility." Born in 1932, Barbara Gittings was a young college student when she decided to learn everything she could about homosexuality. The dearth of information made her haunt libraries, and the lack of community made her form her own. A self-proclaimed joiner and instigator, she began the New York chapter of the first lesbian organization in the United States, the Daughters of Bilitis, and later edited its national magazine *The Ladder*. In the mid-1960s, risking physical harm and loss of employment, she and a small band of protesters picketed Independence Hall in her hometown of Philadelphia, and continued to do so every Fourth of July for five years. After Stonewall emboldened "my people," she successfully joined with other activists to lobby the American Psychiatric Association to rescind its definition of homosexuality as a mental disorder. An advocate for LGBTQ literature, she founded the American Library Association's Gay Task Force, the first professional LGBTQ organization. She died in 2007, survived by her partner of 46 years, Kay Tobin Lahusen.

PRESS

THE *ADVOCATE, LADDER, HOMOSEXUAL CITIZEN, DRUM,* AND *VECTOR* reflected an increasingly strident demand for gay and lesbian rights in the mid-to-late 1960s. This trend exploded in the period following the 1969 Stonewall Riots, unleashing a tidal wave of unapologetic LGBTQ journalism. *GAY* in New York, *Gay Sunshine* in San Francisco, *Gay Liberator* in Detroit, *Killer Dyke* in Chicago, and *Washington Blade* in Washington, D.C., were just a few of the 150 publications being produced by 1972 with an aggregate circulation surpassing 100,000. The publications influenced and reflected a liberated community with their frank language, outrage over LGBTQ discrimination, and celebration of self-expression and open sexuality.

Gay Sunshine was indicative of the bold LGBTQ press of the era.

1948 –

JEANNE CÓRDOVA

IN 1966, JEANNE CÓRDOVA ENTERED THE Immaculate Heart of Mary convent in Santa Barbara, California, but began questioning her sexual orientation and the church's anti-lesbian stance. She left the convent and committed herself to the Los Angeles gay rights and feminist movements. She became president of the Los Angeles chapter of the Daughters of Bilitis, founded the lesbian-feminist publication *The Lesbian Tide*, and became a columnist and human rights editor for the *Los Angeles Free Press*. In 1973, she was a key organizer of what became the largest lesbian conference of the time, and in 1981, founded the *Community Yellow Pages*, the nation's largest and most comprehensive LGBTQ directory.

In 1967, Craig Rodwell opened the first LGBTQ bookstore, The Oscar Wilde Bookshop in New York, to promote the rich and millennial-old heritage of LGBTQ culture and identities. The bookstore soon became an alternative to the bar as a center for LGBTQ gatherings and for the exchange of information. New York's first gay pride march in 1970 was organized out of Rodwell's bookstore.

An LGBTQ literary movement blossomed in the 1970s. Among the great books of the era, Jonathan Ned Katz's *Gay American History* published in 1976 led to a cavalcade of LGBTQ historical texts. Although the LGBTQ bookstore was often the only place to find LGBTQ literature, a few lesbian and gay books crossed over to mainstream booksellers. Patricia Nell Warren's *The Front Runner*, Rita Mae Brown's *Rubyfruit Jungle*, Armistead Maupin's *Tales of the City*, and Andrew Holleran's *Dancer from the Dance* proved that gay and lesbian literature could have success with mainstream audiences.

AUDRE LORDE 1934 – 1992

POET AUDRE LORDE WAS A PIONEER of intersectionality. She insisted on recognition of herself as black, feminist, and lesbian. After completing a degree in library science, Lorde went on to lecture at several universities, write volumes of poetry, and co-found the feminist Kitchen Table: Woman of Color Press. From 1991 until her death, she was New York State's Poet Laureate. From her essay "The Master's Tools Will Never Dismantle the Master's House": "Those of us who stand outside the circle of this society's definition of acceptable women; those of us who have been forged in the crucibles of difference -- those of us who are poor, who are lesbians, who are Black, who are older -- know that survival is not an academic skill. It is learning how to take our differences and make them strengths."

MEDICINE

SINCE THE EMERGENCE OF psychology as a discipline in the late 1800s, psychologists have debated whether to view homosexuality and gender nonconformity as mental illnesses. In 1952, the American Psychiatric Association (APA) listed homosexuality in the Diagnostic and Statistical Manual of Mental Disorders, giving official sanction to efforts among many mental health professionals to find a cure. In 1957, psychologist Eveyln Hooker published "The Adjustment of the Male Overt Homosexual" which postulated that homosexuality was not an illness but a variant in sexual pattern well within the normal range of human behavior.

Activist Frank Kameny ignited the movement to remove the APA's listing of homosexuality as a mental illness in the mid-1960s. By the late 1960s, radical activists had taken up the fight and were coordinating zaps and protests at APA meetings and against prominent psychiatrists and psychologists across the United States. The combination of these protests with behind-the-scenes negotiations, culminated in the landmark 1973 removal of homosexuality as a mental illness from the Diagnostic and Statistical Manual of Mental Disorders.

The LGBTQ community's long history of mistreatment at the hands of medical and mental health establishments led to the development of LGBTQ-controlled health service providers. The Homophile Community Health Services Center in Boston opened in 1971 as the first legally incorporated, LGBTQ-staffed medical group to cater to LGBTQ people. The Los Angeles Gay Community Services Center opened later in the year, providing social programs as well as medical and mental health services. As the community center template spread, over 130 LGBTQ community-services institutions emerged across the nation. The centers provide a variety of local services, including legal, social, cultural, and educational services with programs for homeless people, youth, families, and seniors.

4

1969 – 1980 PRIDE IN DIVERSITY

[
RELIGIOUS, RACIAL, AND
CULTURAL IDENTITIES

TRANSGENDER ACTIVISM

BISEXUAL VISIBILITY

LESBIAN-FEMINISM
]

PERSONAL STORY

> " 'Sisterhood is Beautiful' was an ideal we strove for in all parts of our lives. "

IT WAS AT KATE'S CABIN DOWN a long rugged country road in southern Oregon where I sipped homemade lemonade, curled up in the big armchair in front of the picture window, and soaked up **all things lesbian**. I read Well of Loneliness and wept, read Edward the Dyke and chuckled, read back issues of Quest and pondered. I listened to their collection of women's music. Meg Christian, Cris Williamson, Alix Dobkin. Every poem, every photograph, every song a new **discovery**.

When I came out two months earlier in San Francisco, that spring of 1975, one of the things that was most important to me was to meet another Asian lesbian, of which there seemed none at the time. Only one name was ever mentioned, but I never got to meet her, someone named Sapphire, before I left California to live on womens' land. And then one hot afternoon a big boat of a car came up the road and an Asian woman emerged looking for Kate. Suddenly I found myself looking face to face and exchanging words with this woman in a moment strange—not only because this was the only other Asian face I'd ever seen in the whole state—but because I found her beauty undeniably captivating. At once I knew that this was Sapphire.

Still being so new to lesbians, every time I met some it was an event of note and aroused great anticipation, fear, and **excitement**. Sapphire was an imposing figure with a stunning mane of thick, lustrous black hair that swept down the length of her back. Her presence commanded attention. (Actually I am taller than Sapphire but low cabin ceilings and my sense of invisibility led me to believe that all lesbians I met that summer were taller and bigger than they were).

I thought we'd have an instant rapport based on our common upbringing in the San Francisco Chinese-American community, based on the voluminous reading I'd done about lesbian feminism… about **the Movement**… reading poetry about us being common loaves and an army of lovers. The concept 'Sisterhood is Beautiful' was an ideal we strove for in all parts of our lives. I had harbored secret hopes that I'd find in Sapphire a fascinating, powerful, older Asian sister to look up to… or at least make a friendly acquaintance with.

– Canyon Sam

DEFINITION OF TERMS

In the 1970s, gay replaced homosexual as the term of choice from within the community. Initially, gay was predominantly used as an umbrella term meaning both gay and lesbian people. When the phrases gay rights movement and gay liberation movement are used, it refers to the fight for gay and lesbian rights. As the 1970s progressed, lesbian activists preferred to be identified as lesbians, rather than gay or gay women. Outside of the broader meaning of the term gay in "gay rights movement" and "gay liberation movement" or in organizational names from the 1970s (such as the Gay Liberation Front and National Gay Task Force), when the term gay is used in this text it refers specifically to gay men.

Although the term LGBTQ (lesbian, gay, bisexual, transgender, and queer) has been used throughout the text, it is not a term people used in 1970s. Transgender and bisexual activism emerged in the 1970s, but each functioned on the outskirts of the gay liberation movement. In fact, in this era, transgender and bisexual activists often faced discrimination from gay and lesbian communities. Transgender is used in this text as an umbrella term that covers all people whose gender identity, expression, or behavior differs from those typically associated with the sex they were at birth. Queer was considered a derogatory term in the 1970s, unlike the positive all-inclusive meaning it has today.

RELIGIOUS, RACIAL, AND CULTURAL IDENTITIES

Older gay and lesbian people founded Senior Action in Gay Environment (SAGE) in 1977, the first organization of its kind in the United States. Pictured here is the 1979 opening of the Society for Senior Gay and Lesbian Citizens at their new home at the Los Angeles Gay and Lesbian Center.

IN THE LOS ANGELES SUBURB of Huntington Park in 1968, Troy Perry started the first LGBTQ ministry in the United States, the Metropolitan Community Church. Despite homophobic attacks, the congregation grew from 12 members in 1969 to 43,000 members in almost 300 congregations in 22 countries by the 21st century. Father Patrick X. Nidorf opened the first ministry for LGBTQ Catholics, DignityUSA, in Southern California in 1969. By 1972, the organization had members in twenty states and chapters in ten cities. Beth Chayim Chadashim became the world's first LGBTQ synagogue when it started services in Los Angeles in 1972. The rapid proliferation of LGBTQ synagogues across the world led to the first World Congress of GLBT Jews in 1975. In 1974, Louie Crew began the newsletter *Integrity* for gay and lesbian members of the Episcopalian Church, resulting in the opening of a handful of Integrity chapters across the United States. In 1977, Matthew Price helped found Affirmation—Gay Mormons United, with early chapters in Salt Lake City, Denver, and Dallas. By 1979, chapters in Washington, D.C., Los Angeles, San Francisco, and Salt Lake City had helped to create a national charter and newsletter.

In the post-Stonewall era, racially and culturally identified groups also emerged. In 1970, Third World Gay Revolution groups started in New York and Chicago, and Unidos, a Los Angeles organization for gay Latino Americans, held its first meeting. In 1974, African-American and Latina-American lesbians in New York founded Salsa Soul Sisters as a social alternative to the discriminatory bar scene. In 1975, Randy Burns, a Northern Paiute, and Barbara Cameron, a Lakota Sioux, founded Gay American Indians. San Francisco's Asian-American Alliance and Boston Asian Gay Men and Lesbians were founded in the late 1970s. Other groups of the era include the Native American Gay Rap Group (1972), Gay Latino Alliance/GALA (1975), Third World Lesbian Caucus (1977), and Black Gay Caucus (1977). The National Coalition of Black Gays emerged in 1978 and sponsored the Third World Lesbian and Gay Conference in 1979, bringing together a coalition of racially and culturally identified groups.

TROY PERRY, A PENTECOSTAL MINISTER, moved to California after being expelled from his Tennessee congregation because he was gay. Adrift and despondent, Perry was inspired by a police raid of a local gay bar to create "a church for all of us who are outcast." In October 1968, in the living room of his rented house, Perry conducted the first service of the Metropolitan Community Church (MCC). Membership expanded rapidly, and in 1971 the church purchased property of its own, the first openly LGBTQ organization to do so.

The expansion of church membership gave Perry a pulpit through which to mobilize LGBTQ people for equal rights. He led effective protests on the discriminatory policies of local businesses, police, and government. Perry went on hunger strikes to raise money and awareness for important causes such as the fight against California Proposition 6 (the initiative proposed to fire gay and lesbian educators from public schools). He performed some of the nation's first public gay wedding ceremonies in 1969.

Perry was a national figure within the LGBTQ rights movement. He helped to establish the National New Orleans Memorial Fund to provide medical assistance and support services to victims of a fire that killed 32 people at a New Orleans gay bar that housed MCC church services. In 1977, he participated in the first gay and lesbian coalition to meet at the White House. Perry took a train across the country to encourage support for the 1979 National March on Washington, and in the process brought the LGBTQ movement to previously isolated communities. He performed mass wedding ceremonies at that March on Washington and repeated the act in subsequent marches.

TROY PERRY

1940 –

TRANSGENDER ACTIVISM

Angela Douglas and the Los Angeles Gay Liberation Front picket a bar in 1969 for its posting of the sign "Fagots Stay Out."

IN 1970, TRANSGENDER ACTIVISTS Sylvia Rivera and Marsha P. Johnson broke from New York's Gay Activists Alliance to start the Street Transvestite Action Revolution (STAR). STAR advocated for transgender rights and opened STAR House to provide shelter for transgender youths at risk. In Los Angeles, Angela Douglas founded the Transsexual/Transvestite Action Organization (TAO). TAO opened chapters across the United States and published the national magazine *Mirage* to advocate for transgender rights. However by the end of the decade, STAR, TAO, and the

SYLVIA RIVERA 1951 – 2002

TRANSGENDER WOMAN SYLVIA RIVERA WORKED and lived on the streets of New York City and was subject to frequent violence and police brutality. When the police stormed the Stonewall Inn in 1969, Rivera took an active part in the resistance. She became one of the founding members of the New York Gay Liberation Front and an early member of the Gay Activists Alliance (GAA). Finding GAA dismissive to the cause of transgender people, she co-founded the Street Transvestite Action Revolutionaries (STAR) with Marsha P. Johnson. However, the organization folded two years later, and by the end of the decade, Rivera was back living on the streets. The Sylvia Rivera Law Project was established after her death to "guarantee that all people are free to self-determine their gender identity and expression, regardless of income or race, and without facing harassment, discrimination or violence."

leading transgender-advocacy organization, Erickson Educational Foundation, had folded. Although small community groups persisted, discrimination against transgender people, both from within and outside the gay and lesbian communities, would keep transgender men and women from broader visibility and civil rights mobilization until the early 1990s.

By the 1970s, numerous universities and private doctors had formed gender identity clinics to conduct reassignment surgeries. Fearful of abuse by unqualified practitioners, a group of clinicians, therapists, and researchers began forming standards for care at the yearly International Symposiums on Gender Identity. The Harry Benjamin International Gender Dysphoria Association (HBIGDA), formed in 1979, gave official sanction to standardized procedures for reassignment treatments.

The increase in reassignment surgeries led to a surge of requests for changing the listed gender on government-issued identification cards. When the legal rulings on those requests conflicted with one another, it demonstrated the difficulties judges had in interpreting cases regarding gender nonconformity. In 1977, the successful legal challenge by transgender woman Renée Richards to play professional tennis on the women's circuit, pointed to an improving understanding of gender identity, although it would be some time before municipalities, states, and the judicial system consistently provided some measure of equality.

BISEXUAL VISIBILITY

THE MODERN CONCEPT OF bisexuality gained the nation's attention in Alfred Kinsey's research of the 1940s and 1950s in which he found widespread indications of bisexuality within the United States population. In 1963, Jefferson Poland and Lee Koch started the Sexual Freedom League, one of the first bisexually-oriented groups. In 1964 in New York, the Sexual Freedom League collaborated with gay activists in the first known LGBTQ protest. In 1965, Poland moved from New York to San Francisco where the league's activities garnered broad media coverage.

In 1972, New York bisexual activists formed the National Bisexual Liberation Group, one of the first known groups expressly for bisexuals, and published one of the first known bisexual newsletters, *The Bisexual Expression*. This was followed by the Bisexual Forum in New York in 1974, the San Francisco Bisexual Center in 1976, and ByWays in Chicago in 1978. In 1972, at the annual Friends General Conference in Ithaca, a subgroup of bisexual Quakers wrote the "Ithaca Statement on Bisexuality" and published it in the Quaker's *Friends Journal* and the LGBTQ periodical the *Advocate*, raising bisexual awareness and consciousness.

LESBIAN FEMINISM

IN 1970, THE LESBIAN FEMINIST MOVEMENT came into prominence at the second Congress to Unite Women. Forty lesbian women wearing "Lavender Menace" T-shirts seized the conference and forced an open dialogue about lesbians in the feminist movement. The Lavender Menace women took the name Radicalesbians and, along with groups such as the Lesbian Feminist Liberation, advocated for lesbian rights and liberation. Reversing course from earlier hostilities against lesbian members, National Organization for Women (NOW) delegates at the 1971 national conference approved a resolution recognizing a woman's right to define her own sexuality and lifestyle.

Building on the success of the first West Coast Lesbian Conference in 1971, Jeanne Córdova invited lesbians from around the world to a second conference in 1973. With over 2,000 in attendance, the conference was the largest gathering of lesbians to that date.

Lesbian feminists opened their own bookstores, restaurants, and softball leagues to create a supportive community independent from patriarchal and heteronormative society. Amazon Bookstore opened in Minneapolis in 1970 to become the nation's first known feminist bookstore. Women's spaces such as the Woman's Building in Los Angeles were founded as exclusively female centers of art and culture. By 1975, some 50 lesbian publications circulated to tens of thousands of readers across the United States. Women's presses such as Diana Press, Naiad, Clothespin Fever Press, Daughters Inc., and Kitchen Table: Women of Color Press brought pro-feminist, pro-lesbian books to the market. Olivia Records opened in 1973 and quickly became the leader in producing women's music. Building on the success of regional festivals, the National Women's Music Festival in 1974 and the Michigan Womyn's Music Festival in 1976 launched to become two of the more successful music events to celebrate feminist and lesbian musicians and the separatist ethos.

Pride in Diversity

Bisexual artist Kate Millet (in white) with feminist Wiccan Zoe Budapest at the National Lesbian Conference in 1973.

5

RESPONSE TO ADVERSITY

1973 – 1980

[BACKLASH

NATIONAL LEVEL ACTIVISM]

Protesters against Anita Bryant and the discriminatory California Proposition 6, the Briggs Initiative.

BACKLASH

AS OPENLY LGBTQ INSTITUTIONS multiplied in the early 1970s, their emerging voice and visibility made them targets of a series of arson attacks. Arsonists targeted Metropolitan Community Church buildings in Nashville and San Francisco and burnt down the mother church in Los Angeles. Arson fires and bomb attacks destroyed gay bars in San Francisco and Springfield, Massachusetts. Fires claimed LGBTQ services and activists buildings in Phoenix, Buffalo, and New York. In the

Harvey Milk

1930 – 1978

HARVEY MILK HAD BEEN A SCHOOLTEACHER, insurance company actuary, financial clerk, and Wall Street analyst before moving to San Francisco and becoming a leading figure in the gay rights movement. He ran for a seat on the San Francisco Board of Supervisors in 1973 and again in 1975, before winning in the 1977 election. He became the first openly LGBTQ person to be elected for public office in California.

Milk spearheaded the passing of a city-wide anti-discrimination bill for LGBTQ people. He fought against Proposition 6 to ban LGBTQ teachers from schools, and debated State Senator John Briggs, the proposition's sponsor, across the state. For many, Milk and his call for all gay and lesbian people to come out of the closet, was the face of the campaign and a main factor in the proposition's defeat.

On November 27, 1978, former supervisor Dan White assassinated Harvey Milk and Mayor George Moscone in their offices. Memorial services culminated in more than 25,000 people carrying candles in a silent march from the Castro district to city hall. The 1979 March on Washington was organized in part as a way to honor Milk's legacy.

worst catastrophe, thirty-two men died in the arson fire of the UpStairs Lounge bar in New Orleans that doubled as the home for the local Metropolitan Community Church.

In 1977, a conservative uprising headed by singer Anita Bryant fought to roll back LGBTQ equal rights legislation. Their "Save Our Children" campaign helped to reverse equal rights legislation in Dade County, Florida; St. Paul, Minnesota; Wichita, Kansas; and Eugene, Oregon. In California, State Senator John Briggs sponsored Proposition 6, a measure to purge LGBTQ teachers from public schools and prohibit the positive discussion of homosexuality. Municipal Elections Committee of Los Angeles (MECLA), San Francisco Supervisor Harvey Milk, and activists like Troy Perry, Ivy Bottini, Morris Kight, and Jeanne Córdova led a campaign to defeat the measure at the polls, and won by a 2 to 1 margin.

The assassination of Harvey Milk led to a massive candlelight march in San Francisco to honor the LGBTQ leader.

But the success was marred by tragedy when later that year, San Francisco Mayor George Moscone and Supervisor Harvey Milk were assassinated in their offices. The first openly LGBTQ elected official in California, Harvey Milk had become a hero in the community for his outspoken leadership for LGBTQ rights. When assassin Dan White received a lenient 7-year sentence for the murders, the largest LGBTQ riot ever recorded broke out on the streets of San Francisco. Police retaliated against the LGBTQ community by raiding the streets and bars of the heavily LGBTQ-populated Castro District, clubbing citizens and destroying property. An agreement between LGBTQ activists and city leaders ceased the violence and led to a peaceful gathering of 10,000 people on Castro Street to commemorate the fallen leader on what would have been his 49th birthday.

NATIONAL LEVEL ACTIVISM

IN THE 1970S, LGBTQ ACTIVISTS sought to build a national movement for LGBTQ rights. In 1973, the National Gay Task Force formed as an advocate for LGBTQ rights, modeled after the American Civil Liberties Union. The Lambda Legal Defense and Education Fund was established the same year, becoming the nation's first LGBTQ legal organization. To bring more political pressure to LGBTQ rights issues, the Gay Rights National Lobby was founded in 1976 and the Human Rights Campaign Fund in 1980. The two organizations would eventually merge to become the largest civil rights organization advocating for LGBTQ Americans. Horizons Foundation, Gay Rights Advocates, Lesbian Rights Project, and Gay and Lesbian Advocates and Defenders, emerged at the end of the decade to the join the national effort.

In 1979, a massive march on Washington demonstrated the great diversity of people and organizations that had arisen in the decade following the Stonewall riots. The march celebrated the LGBTQ movement's significant achievements in local communities, its success against sodomy laws at the state level, and the promise of a great coalition at the national level. The march also addressed how much left there was to achieve. There was still no federal or state anti-discrimination legislation for LGBTQ citizens. There were no same-sex partner benefits, even on the municipal level. Challenges against bans on same-sex marriage and gay and lesbian participation in military service had yet to achieve any success.

STEVE ENDEAN 1948 – 1993

INSPIRED BY THE GAY RIGHTS ADVOCACY of Jack Baker and Mike McConnell, Steve Endean joined the gay rights cause while a student at the University of Minnesota. He formed the one-man Gay Rights Lobby and used it to usher through a broad anti-discrimination bill in Minneapolis in 1973. He moved to Washington, D.C., and took over the ailing Gay Rights National Lobby in 1978. Endean focused his efforts on lobbying the United States Congress for a gay and lesbian anti-discrimination bill. Understanding that money means political power, he helped found, then lead, the Human Rights Campaign Fund in 1980.

Response to Adversity

The Immigration and Naturalization Service still excluded LGBTQ people from entering the country. For all that was built and achieved in a decade, the LGBTQ movement would have to continue the struggle into the following decades for broader civil rights victories.

A crowd gathers at the 1979 March on Washington for Lesbian and Gay Rights, the LGBTQ community's first national march for civil rights.

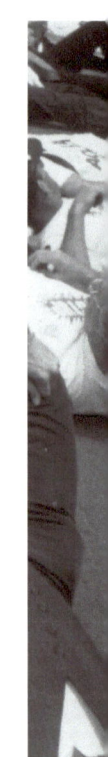

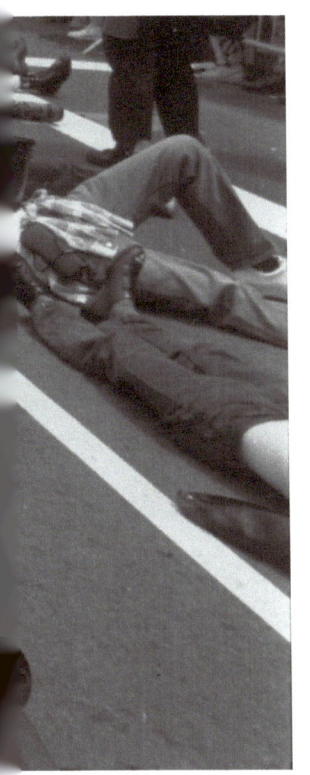

THE AIDS ERA

1981 – 1993

[AIDS
BENEFITS AND FAMILY
MARCH ON WASHINGTON
BISEXUAL ACTIVISM]

The AIDS Era

PERSONAL STORY

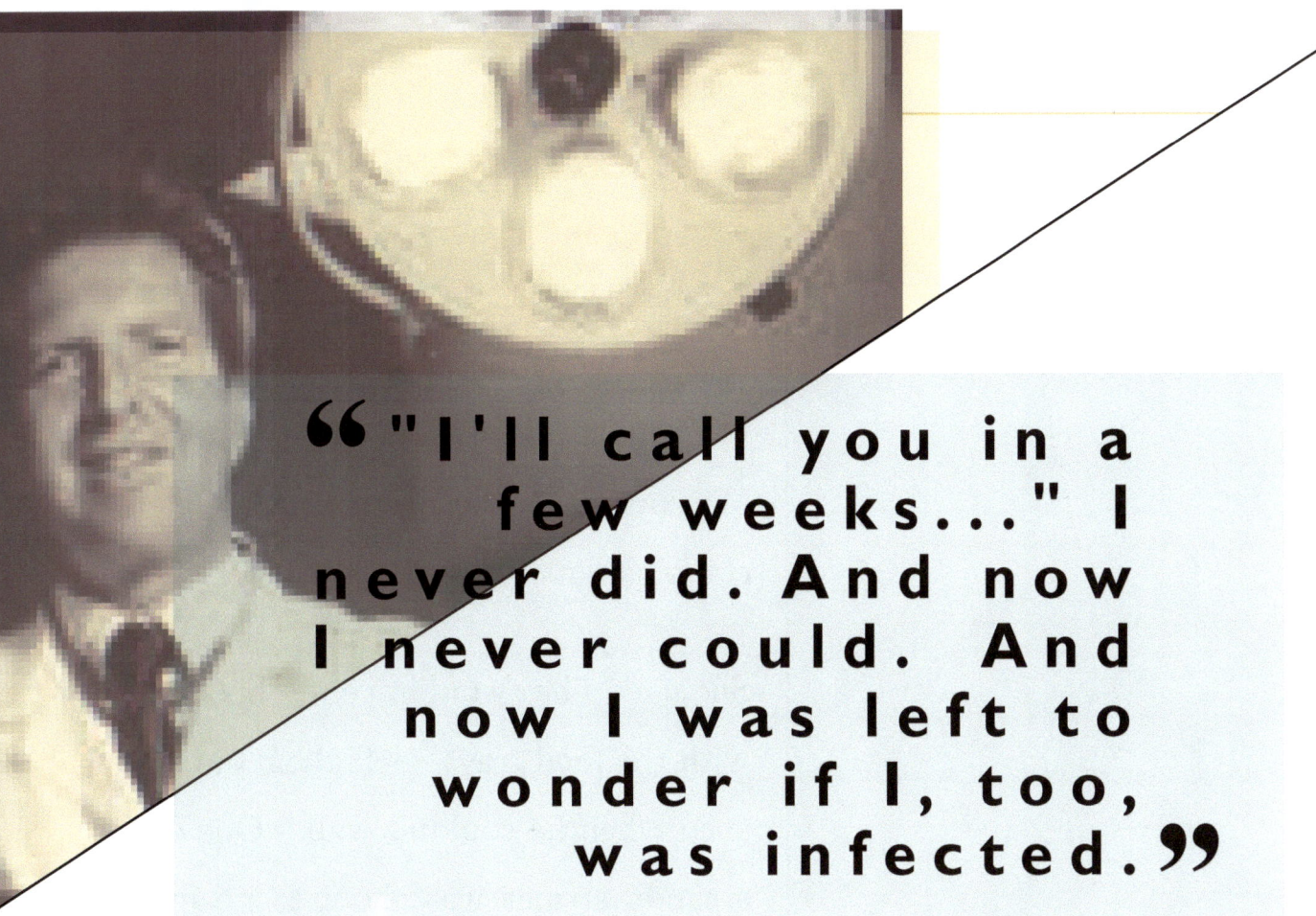

> "I'll call you in a few weeks..." I never did. And now I never could. And now I was left to wonder if I, too, was infected."

I moved to Los Angeles in early 1985 from Wisconsin; 4 years into the epidemic I did not know a person with **HIV or AIDS**. Soon, I was thrust into the world of hearing terms on a daily basis, from friends and patients alike, such as "I've been diagnosed," or "He's got the pneumonia," and seeing purplish Kaposi's sarcoma lesions everywhere I went in Los Angeles.

I remember specifically when my sister called to tell me about that Enrique, someone I had **dated** while living in Wisconsin, had died from AIDS-related complications. It was October of 1985.

She said "They wouldn't enter his room with the food trays—left them outside even when he couldn't walk. One day a candy striper was about to go in— Enrique was waving a dollar bill at her through the glass window; he wanted a candy bar. Well, a nurse ran over to the striper, whispered something, and moments later the girl pushed her cart quickly down the hall."

The AIDS Era

"Enrique never got to tell his mother he was dying—who knows if he even knew he was dying?" my sister went on. "He phoned his mother to say that he had a **bad flu** and was going in to the hospital to rest for a few days. He had even promised to come to San Juan to see her for Thanksgiving."

I remembered that last phone call Enrique and I had exchanged the previous December, just before I had moved. He had asked me if I thought all the diarrhea and weight loss he was experiencing could be due to "that new awful AIDS I've been hearing about."

> "Come on, Enrique. I'm sure it'll pass. You're fine, **just a bug** or something. I'll call you in a few weeks after I'm settled."
>
> I never did. And now I never could. And now I was left to wonder if I, too, was infected.
>
> – Dr. Mark Katz

DEFINITION OF TERMS

Although the term LGBTQ (lesbian, gay, bisexual, transgender, and queer) has been used throughout the text, it is not a term people used in the 1980s. Queer remained a derogatory term, although the term had started to be reclaimed by the LGBTQ community by the end of the decade. The rise of GLB or LGB acronyms at the end of this era signaled bisexuals as an increasing part of the gay and lesbian coalition. Transgender activism was not prominent in the 1980s and transgender people still struggled for acceptance within the gay, lesbian, and bisexual communities. Transgender activism would not emerge as a force and enter into broader coalition until later in the 1990s.

The AIDS Era

AIDS

THE FIRST CASES OF WHAT would later be termed Acquired Immune Deficiency Syndrome (AIDS) were reported in 1981 when young men in three major United States cities were hospitalized with cases of extremely rare, deadly opportunistic infections. Within fifteen years, AIDS would become the leading cause of death for Americans aged 25-44.

Now it is known that the human immunodeficiency virus (HIV), the virus that causes AIDS, is a blood-borne, sexually transmitted disease that cannot be acquired via casual contact. But in the early 1980s, all anyone knew was that this new illness was fatal. The ambiguity was a recipe for panic and blame.

Because the first reported cases of disease were among gay men, public opinion pigeonholed the burgeoning epidemic as a "gay plague." The stigma of homosexuality remained strong in the 1980s, a decade which began with no federal or statewide anti-discrimination laws in place to protect the civil rights of LGBTQ people. This prejudice seemed to be a primary cause of the relative inaction of the federal government to address the epidemic. From June 1981 to June 1982, the Centers for Disease Control and Prevention (CDC) spent $1 million on AIDS, which by October 1982, had stricken 634 Americans and killed 260. Across the same time frame, the CDC spent $9 million on Legionnaires'

1935 – 2020   L A R R Y   K R A M E R

A NOVELIST AND ACADEMY AWARD-NOMINATED screenwriter, Larry Kramer saw early on that AIDS would devastate the gay male population. He cofounded one of the first organizations to confront the epidemic, Gay Men's Health Crisis, and five years later helped form the more combative collective, AIDS Coalition to Unleash Power (ACT UP). Kramer realized that protesting against drug companies had to be made visually interesting in order to garner the media coverage ACT UP sought as leverage for policy change. ACT UP's theatrical protests and arresting graphics provided the gay community a voice in determining how to treat a disease which overwhelmingly affected themselves. Kramer went on to write a prize-winning Broadway play about the early days of AIDS, *The Normal Heart*.

By 1985, media rhetoric concerning those with AIDS highlighted the "innocent victims" of the disease, meaning babies born ill or hemophiliacs infected via blood transfusion. The Gay and Lesbian Alliance Against Defamation (GLAAD) formed partly to combat the widespread notion that gay men with HIV were, conversely, somehow to blame for their own deaths. They compiled instances of homophobic statements and depictions in media portrayals, news reports, and political rhetoric. Readers of GLAAD's newsletter were given addresses of producers, publishers, and politicians responsible for bigoted language or portrayals, and were encouraged to make their voice heard. This picture shows a GLAAD protest at a movie studio in Los Angeles.

disease, which had caused fewer than 50 deaths. Even more troubling, because of the long incubation period, it was estimated that a quarter of a million Americans were infected by the time of the first deaths.

Some gay men reacted to the sudden appearance of AIDS in the community with denial. Scant public health warnings and virtually absent media attention gave rise to theories that the new disease didn't actually exist or couldn't be spread by sexual contact. The early inability of scientists to find the cause of the disease contributed to the confusion. Doctors and activists who spoke of a coming cataclysm were distrusted and dismissed for exaggerating the threat. Many gay men felt that authorities were trying to put them back in the closet and reverse the hard-won battles for acceptance and visibility.

This perception was heightened by homophobic rhetoric from religious and government leaders in the early years of the epidemic. Future White House Communications Director Pat Buchanan wrote: "The poor homosexuals -- they have declared war upon nature, and now nature is extracting an awful retribution." Moral Majority leader Reverend Jerry Falwell said: "AIDS is not just God's punishment for homosexuals; it is God's punishment for the society that tolerates homosexuals." *The New York Times* published conservative leader William F. Buckley's call for people with AIDS to be tattooed for identification purposes.

Public opinion tended to blame those with AIDS for the disease. Hemophiliac children infected through blood transfusions were forced to leave school. A backlash of fear intensified after movie star Rock Hudson, one of the first public figures to confirm his diagnosis, died from

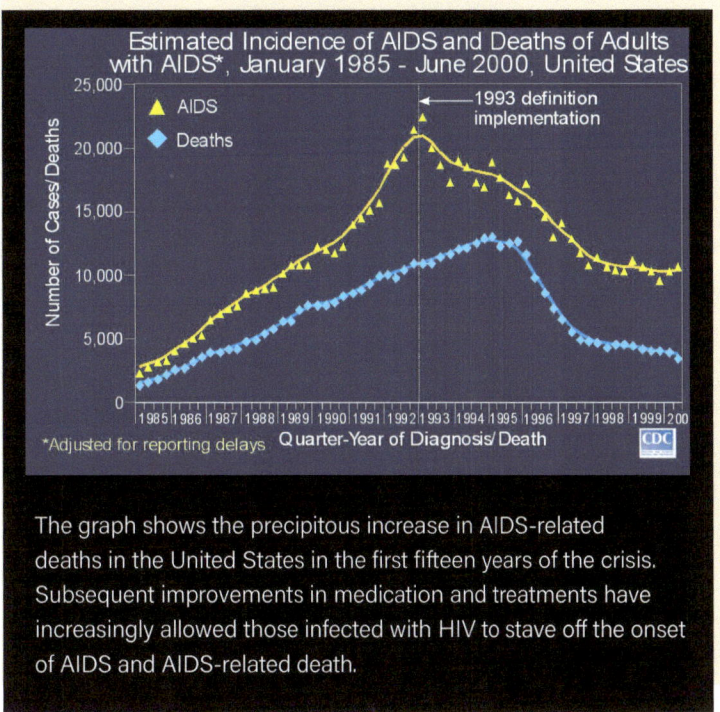

The graph shows the precipitous increase in AIDS-related deaths in the United States in the first fifteen years of the crisis. Subsequent improvements in medication and treatments have increasingly allowed those infected with HIV to stave off the onset of AIDS and AIDS-related death.

URVASHI VAID
1958 –

URVASHI VAID WAS HIRED OUT OF LAW SCHOOL by the American Civil Liberties Union, where as part of the National Prisons Project, she worked for the rights of prisoners who were HIV-positive. In 1986, she joined the National Gay and Lesbian Task Force (NGLTF) and served for three years as the public information director. In 1989, she became NGLTF's executive director, the first person of color to head a mainstream national LGBTQ civil rights organization. She briefly retired to write the award winning *Virtual Equality: The Mainstreaming of Gay and Lesbian Liberation*, before returning to the NGLTF as their public information director. As of 2013, Vaid served as the Deputy Director of the Governance and Civil Society Unit of the Peace and Social Justice Program of the Ford Foundation.

complications of AIDS in 1985. *Life* magazine screamed on its cover, "Now no one is safe from AIDS." Violence against gay men rose precipitously.

In 1986, right-wing political activist Lyndon LaRouche crafted California Proposition 64, which would give the state the power to quarantine those with HIV. The initiative collected near 700,000 signatures, twice the number needed to put the measure on the ballot. LGBTQ activists feared that if they lost, similar initiatives would spread across the United States. Through increasingly sophisticated political organizing, fundraising, and grassroots operations, LGBTQ activists were able to deliver an overwhelming defeat of the measure at the polls.

Scientists at the CDC and other institutions in the United States and France eventually determined that the retrovirus HIV caused a breakdown of the body's immune system. A test for the virus became available in 1985. With confirmation that the disease could be spread by sex, the gay community—the hardest hit, but by no means the only population at risk—reorganized to meet the crisis.

Groups such as Gay Men's Health Crisis, Project Inform, AIDS Project Los Angeles, and the American Foundation for AIDS Research, formed to fill the void of effective public health policy by raising money for research and education, and to support those with the disease. However, the mounting

VIRGINIA APUZZO 1941 –

AFTER THREE YEARS AS A NUN, Virginia Apuzzo decided to pursue her political interests. She argued for a gay rights plank in the 1976 Democratic National Committee platform and joined the Women's Caucus of the National Gay Task Force (NGTF). In 1982, she became Executive Director of NGTF and directed the organization to push for a federal response to AIDS. In 1985, she joined New York Governor Mario Cuomo's administration, where she worked on the Consumer Protection Board to challenge pharmaceutical companies over pricing of AIDS drugs and to change discriminatory policies in the insurance industry. Once arrested outside the White House as a protester against the Reagan administration's lack of response to AIDS, she became the highest-ranking openly LGBTQ person in the Clinton Administration where she secured fast-track disability benefits for those with the disease. "For a long time gays' objective was to get government off our backs. With the advent of AIDS it became very clear that there were some problems the government had to be involved in."

The AIDS Era

The AIDS Coalition to Unleash Power (ACT UP) formed in New York City in 1987 under the motto: "United in anger and committed to direct action to end the AIDS crisis." Symbolized by a pink triangle and the slogan "SILENCE=DEATH," the group operated through a radical democratic decision-by-consensus style. They became known for their disruptive protests, theatrical street demonstrations, and willingness to be arrested for their cause. At their height, they boasted thousands of members in chapters across the United States and spawned such groups as the artists collective Gran Fury, the militant Queer Nation, and the Treatment Action Group (TAG). TAG's medical expertise worked alongside ACT UP's activism to reform the drug trial policies and speed the development of new drugs in the Food and Drug Administration. Their work changed the way this and future epidemics were to be handled by governmental and corporate entities. By 1996, advances in antiviral therapies allowed HIV/AIDS to be largely managed and transformed it from the death sentence that it had been for the previous fifteen years.

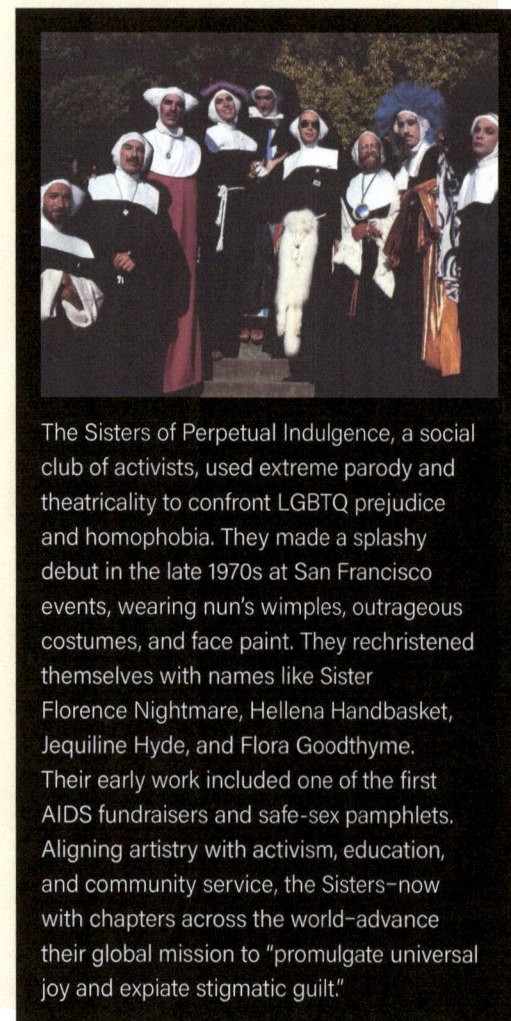

The Sisters of Perpetual Indulgence, a social club of activists, used extreme parody and theatricality to confront LGBTQ prejudice and homophobia. They made a splashy debut in the late 1970s at San Francisco events, wearing nun's wimples, outrageous costumes, and face paint. They rechristened themselves with names like Sister Florence Nightmare, Hellena Handbasket, Jequiline Hyde, and Flora Goodthyme. Their early work included one of the first AIDS fundraisers and safe-sex pamphlets. Aligning artistry with activism, education, and community service, the Sisters–now with chapters across the world–advance their global mission to "promulgate universal joy and expiate stigmatic guilt."

death toll and sheer scale of the epidemic overwhelmed the meager resources of grassroots organizations. The federal government needed to become involved. Coming out in support of increased funding for AIDS research meant personal visibility and vulnerability in a society in which one could be legally fired or evicted for being LGBTQ. But a life-and-death desperation in the gay community drove increasing numbers to take the risk.

Isolated acts of protest in 1985 and 1986, and increasingly combative reports in gay publications, indicated the mounting anger in the gay community. In early 1987, the Center for Disease Control convened a conference about the question of routine AIDS testing of certain populations. A protest group calling itself the Lavender Hill Mob stormed the proceedings and shouted down the speakers, pleading for the scientific community to "test drugs, not people." The Mob dressed distinctively – they wore the pink triangle insignia forced upon gay men in Nazi concentration camps. Avram Finkelstein's Silence=Death collective spread posters throughout New York City to foment expanded gay activism.

The AIDS Coalition to Unleash Power (ACT UP) formed in 1987 and quickly became the face of the new activism. A primary target of the group was the availability of medications. Drugs identified as promising for AIDS treatment had not been fast-tracked for testing by the Food and Drug Administration (FDA). The sole drug available was a failed cancer drug that cost thousands of dollars a year,

The AIDS Era

and clinical trial protocols denied patients potential alternatives. Using civil disobedience, direct-action tactics, and media visibility, ACT UP put pressure on the FDA to expedite their work.

The federal government response was slow. By 1987, when President Reagan gave his first policy speech about AIDS, nearly forty thousand Americans had been diagnosed with the disease and over twenty thousand had died. That same year, Congress adopted an amendment banning funds for any AIDS education materials that "promote or encourage, directly or indirectly, homosexual activities." This effectively outlawed any federally-funded education efforts which mentioned homosexual acts that could spread the virus. At the same time, other nations such as the United Kingdom, Uganda, and Thailand undertook massive educational programs that served as models of HIV prevention.

Reagan's Commission on AIDS eventually released a report urging the protection of those with HIV against discrimination, an expansion of funding and services to fight AIDS, and money for preventive education. These recommendations were allowed to languish. Congress responded in 1988 by approving legislation that would define a comprehensive federal program to fight and treat AIDS. In 1990, the death of a teenager with hemophilia prompted the Ryan White Comprehensive AIDS Resource Emergency (CARE) Act, which funded community-based care and treatment services. The Americans with Disabilities Act of 1990 was the first federal law to offer some protection against discrimination for those with HIV.

1957 – 1994 MARLON RIGGS

AN EMMY- AND PEABODY-AWARD-WINNING documentarian, Marlon Riggs, created films that confronted issues of racism and homophobia. His 1989 documentary, *Tongues Untied*, examined black gay male sexuality, particularly the differences between conceptions of macho and sissy within the black community. Other films include the 1987 documentary *Ethnic Notions* on racial stereotyping; *Color Adjustment: Blacks in Prime Time* (1991) about the stereotypical portrayal of black people on television; *No Regrets* (1993) about five HIV-positive black men addressing the stigma of HIV/AIDS and homosexuality in the black community; and *Black Is...Black Ain't* (released posthumously in 1995) regarding the diversity of black identities.

BENEFITS AND FAMILY

OFTEN DISCUSSED SOLELY IN terms of gay men, AIDS had an impact on lesbians as well. Previously, lesbian and gay people had existed more as side-by-side entities than as one community. The epidemic brought the two together as lesbians cared and fought for ailing gay men.

The influx of AIDS patients to hospitals made acute many of the iniquities faced by same-sex couples. Because same-sex relationships were not legally recognized, hospitals could deny a gay man visitation rights, or say over the health needs of his life-partner dying of AIDS. Upon the death of a partner, the surviving person was also denied the rights and benefits accorded married couples. In 1986, a New York City gay man, Miguel Braschi, was threatened eviction when his partner died of AIDS-related complications. The case was ultimately decided in favor of Braschi. It was the first United States court decision to give any legal protection to same-sex couples.

In 1982, The Village Voice newspaper in New York became the first corporate entity to provide health and other benefits to unmarried partners of employees, and in 1984, the city of Berkeley was the first to offer domestic partnership benefits for public employees. However, these small steps

ROBERTA ACHTENBERG   1950 –

ROBERTA ACHTENBERG GREW UP IN Los Angeles and attended law school in San Francisco. In 1989, she was elected to that city's Board of Supervisors. Three years later, after she spoke at the 1992 National Democratic Convention, President Clinton chose her to be the Assistant Secretary of Housing and Urban Development for Fair Housing and Equal Opportunity. After a bruising United States Senate confirmation battle, she became the first openly LGBTQ presidential appointee. Since completing her work for the federal government, she has served as Chairman of the Board of Trustees of California State University. In 2011, President Obama named her to the United States Commission on Civil Rights.

underscored the vulnerability of the vast majority of committed gay and lesbian couples in this era. Same-sex couples continued to be denied benefits, non-citizens deported over the wishes of their same-sex partner, and children removed from the homes of gay and lesbian parents. Anti-sodomy laws, which were upheld by the 1986 United States Supreme Court decision *Bowers v. Hardwick*, continued to make presumptive criminals of gay and lesbian people and to make an argument against providing them benefits and rights.

MARCH ON WASHINGTON

BY 1987, THE LGBTQ COMMUNITY was angry. The *Bowers v. Hardwick* Supreme Court decision had upheld statutes criminalizing private sexual relations between same-sex partners, and the Reagan Administration's newly formed Commission on AIDS was in serious disarray (its chair and vice-chair resigned within months). In response, a steering committee recruited from LGBTQ organizations nationwide proposed a March on Washington to articulate such demands as the legal recognition of lesbian and

In 1979, Sharon Kowalski and Karen Thompson (pictured above) fell in love and bought a house together. Because there was no legal way for the couple to marry, they named one another as policy beneficiaries to indicate their mutual commitment. Four years later, Kowalski was hit by a drunk driver and rendered incapacitated. Kowalski's father, who refused to acknowledge the relationship between his daughter and her partner, was given guardianship rights. Thompson was prevented from caring for her, and even from seeing her, for several years. It took nearly a decade plus a court appeal before Thompson was declared Kowalski's legal guardian.

gay relationships, the repeal of all laws criminalizing sodomy, an end to discrimination, and massive increases in funding for AIDS education, research, and patient care. On October 11, 1987, the Second National March on Washington for Lesbian and Gay Rights drew roughly a half-million LGBTQ people and their allies, including civil rights leader Cesar Chavez, President of the National Organization for Women Eleanor Smeal, and presidential candidate Jesse Jackson.

The day before the march, Reverend Troy Perry, founder of the Metropolitan Community Church, performed a mass commitment ceremony for thousands of same-sex couples. At dawn on the day of the march, the NAMES Project Foundation AIDS Memorial Quilt was unveiled for the first time. Two days after the march, several hundred demonstrators were arrested outside the Supreme Court while protesting the *Bowers v. Hardwick* decision.

The march had a profound impact on the hundreds of thousands that attended and helped mobilize grassroots organizing across the country. Major national entities that emerged from the march included BiNet USA and the National Latino/a Gay and Lesbian Organization. Robert Eichberg and Jean O'Leary founded National Coming Out Day in 1988, which is held every year on October 11, the anniversary of the march. However, because media outlets largely did not cover LGBTQ events or activism, most of the country never heard about one of the largest civil rights marches in United States history or the deeply moving memorial quilt.

LOU SULLIVAN 1951 – 1991

BORN SHEILA JEAN SULLIVAN, Lou Sullivan joined the Gay People's Union (GPU) at the University of Wisconsin in Milwaukee and soon began writing for the GPU paper on transgender issues. He sought sex reassignment surgery at Stanford University's gender dysphoria program, but was rejected due to the restrictive policies of the era in treating gay-identified individuals. Privatization of the industry and a subsequent loosening of restrictions allowed him to successfully transition in 1980 and begin living full-time as a man. While working at the Janis Information Facility, a transgender referral and information center, he wrote *Information for the Female-to-Male Cross Dresser and Transsexual*, which became standard reading for the female-to-male (FTM) transgender community. In 1986, he started the first FTM-only support group and newsletter. As of 2014, FTM International is the longest-running and largest FTM organization in the world.

The AIDS Era

In the mid-1980s, activist Cleve Jones and fellow demonstrators plastered a wall with placards showing names of San Franciscans who had died of AIDS. To Jones, the effect resembled a quilt. Within two years, he and others had formed the NAMES Project Foundation. The object was to express private grief through traditional craft in a publicly displayed and mobile memorial. The panels allowed individuals, families, and organizations to commemorate a partner, friend, or co-worker whose life was cut short by AIDS.

Shown for the first time in 1987 at the Second National March on Washington for Gay and Lesbian Rights, it contained over nineteen hundred panels. The names commemorated in the panels were read in a ceremony that lasted hours. After the march, it was taken on a four-month tour, during which more panels were added, tripling its size. As of 2020, the quilt includes over 50,000 panels commemorating over 105,000 people who died from AIDS-related causes. The project was the subject of the Academy Award-winning 1989 documentary *Common Threads: Stories from the Quilt*.

BISEXUAL ACTIVISM

IN THE 1980S, BISEXUAL WOMEN formed their own groups to more closely align with feminist principles. Founded in 1983, the Boston Bisexual Women's Network was one of the earliest of these groups. Also in the 1980s, the East Coast Bisexual Network, Bay Area Bisexual Network, and New York Area Bisexual Network—as well as political organizations such as San Francisco's BiPOL, Boston's BiCEP, and New York City's BiPAC—formed demonstrating a broader coalition and reach of bisexual activists.

In conjunction with the 1984 Democratic Convention, BiPOL organized the first rally for bisexual rights. In 1990, the North American Bisexual Network (later called BiNet) formed as the first national organization, and in 1990, BiPOL organized the first U.S. National Bisexual Conference in San Francisco. The second national conference came about in conjunction with the 1993 March on Washington for Lesbian, Gay and Bi Equal Rights and Liberation; the first national march to include bisexuals in the title.

Bisexual visibility, and integration in the LGBTQ movement, continued to grow in the years to follow. Connecticut State Representative Evelyn Mantilla came out in 1997 to become the first openly bisexual elected politician. In 1999, Celebrate Bisexuality Day launched and became an annual celebration on September 23 to celebrate bisexual identity.

The AIDS Era 89

Gilbert Baker is credited for designing the first gay pride flag. The original had eight stripes of color and first flew at San Francisco's pride parade in 1978.

The bisexual flag is credited to a team led by Michael Page. It was influenced by the Biangels symbol and was first flown at the BiCafe in 1998.

Many flags have been raised to represent the transgender community, but this one by Monica Helms, first flown at the 2000 Phoenix pride parade, is probably the most common.

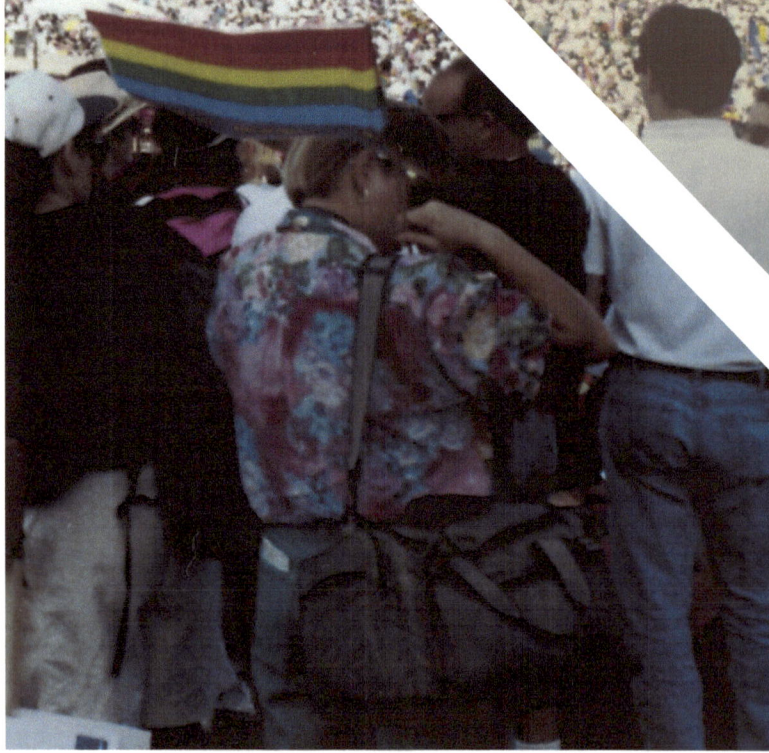

7

THE LGBTQ RIGHTS MOVEMENT

1993 – 2016

[VIOLENCE AND HATE CRIMES

MILITARY SERVICE

DISCRIMINATION

MARRIAGE

TRANSGENDER EQUAL RIGHTS]

PERSONAL STORY

LGBT Rights Movement

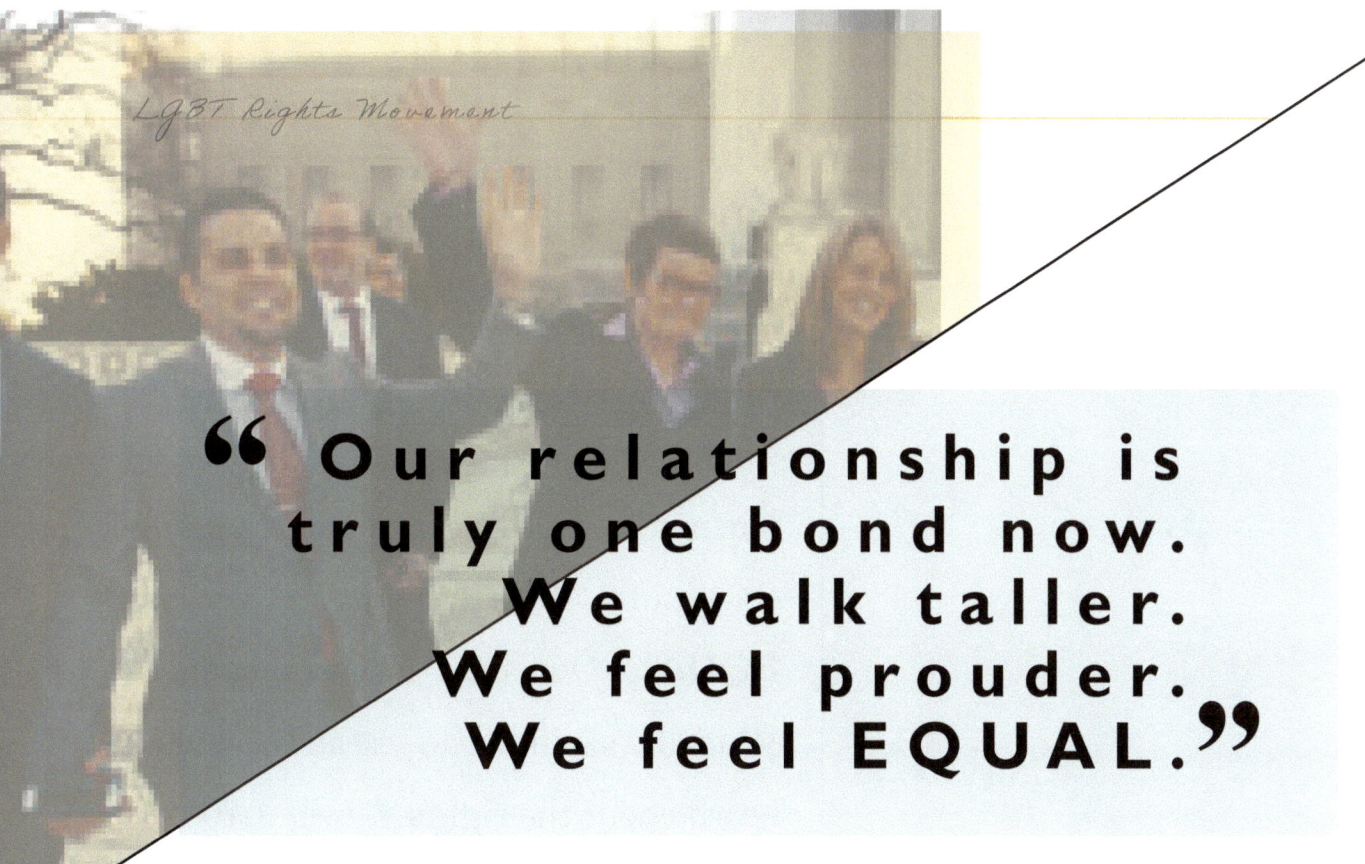

> " Our relationship is truly one bond now. We walk taller. We feel prouder. We feel EQUAL. "

On June 28, 2013, we were the first couple in Los Angeles to get married after the United States Supreme Court held our opponents did not have the legal standing to overturn same-sex **marriage** in California. It was very important for us to get married as soon as it was legal. We had been part of a lawsuit to reinstate same-sex marriage in California for almost 4 ½ years. We had waited long enough.

We were married at 6:08 pm on Friday, June 28, 2013 live on the Rachel Maddow Show. Our four-plus year journey to the altar lasted a whopping six minutes. With two words we became **EQUAL**. Our lives forever changed. What did saying "I do" mean? You have heard about the rights… over 1,100 of them that are denied people who cannot marry. Those are extremely important to the safety and security of gay and lesbian couples.

But do you know what we were most excited about? The access to the language. We couldn't wait to say the words "married" and "husband." These words have true meaning. They are recognized globally. People know what they mean. Our old nicknames for each other have changed. It's now, "husband" this and "husband" that. We can't wait to introduce each other as "husband," sometimes, even to people who already know us because we just want to say the word. We can say unequivocally, "Being married feels different." Look, after 12 plus years together, the day to day hasn't changed much but the feelings have. The love is deeper. The level of **commitment** is stronger. Our relationship is truly one bond now. We walk taller. We feel prouder. We feel EQUAL.

– Paul Katami and Jeff Zarrillo

VIOLENCE AND HATE CRIMES

JAMIE NABOZNY WAS VERBALLY and physically assaulted in school for being gay. When he and his parents complained, school administrators blamed Jamie for the assaults because of his sexual orientation. Jamie attempted suicide, ran away from home, and suffered from post traumatic stress disorder. Eventually Jamie opened a civil suit against his public high school for failing to protect him. In a landmark decision in 1996, the jury ruled that a school could be held accountable for failing to stop anti-LGBTQ abuse.

That case increased accountability for schools to ensure the safety of their LGBTQ students. It led to the nationwide development of sexual orientation anti-harassment policies and programs in schools. Today, GLSEN (Gay, Lesbian & Straight Education Network), PFLAG (Parents, Families and Friends of Lesbians and Gays), and other groups work with schools to support LGBTQ students. Many LGBTQ

The first known efforts to protect LGBTQ youth emerged in the 1970s and 1980s. After hearing the story of a 15-year-old gay teen who was beaten and thrown out of an emergency shelter, Emery Hetrick and Damien Martin founded the Institute for the Protection of Lesbian and Gay Youth (IPLGY) in 1979. Renamed the Hetrick-Martin Institute, the institute established New York's Harvey Milk High School in 1985 for at-risk youth.

Educator Dr. Virginia Uribe (pictured) began Project 10 in 1984 at Los Angeles' Fairfax High as a dropout prevention program for "students who self-identify as gay or lesbian or who express conflicts over sexual orientation." Project 10 grew to include a majority of high schools in the Los Angeles district and is today replicated in districts throughout the country.

LGBT Rights Movement

students take part in an annual Day of Silence, during which they take a vow of silence to raise awareness to the harassment and discrimination that LGBTQ people often suffer in silence.

The Hate Crimes Prevention Act (HCPA) was introduced in Congress in 1997 to expand federal protection to include those subject to a criminal act on the basis of their gender or sexual orientation. HCPA received renewed interest the next year when Matthew Shepard, an openly gay university student, was brutally beaten and left to die in rural Wyoming. In 1999, HCPA was defeated in Congress, but the measure was later reintroduced as the Matthew Shepard and James Byrd, Jr. Hate Crimes Prevention Act, with disability and gender identity added to the list of protected people. The act was signed into law in 2009, becoming the first federal law to offer protection to transgender people.

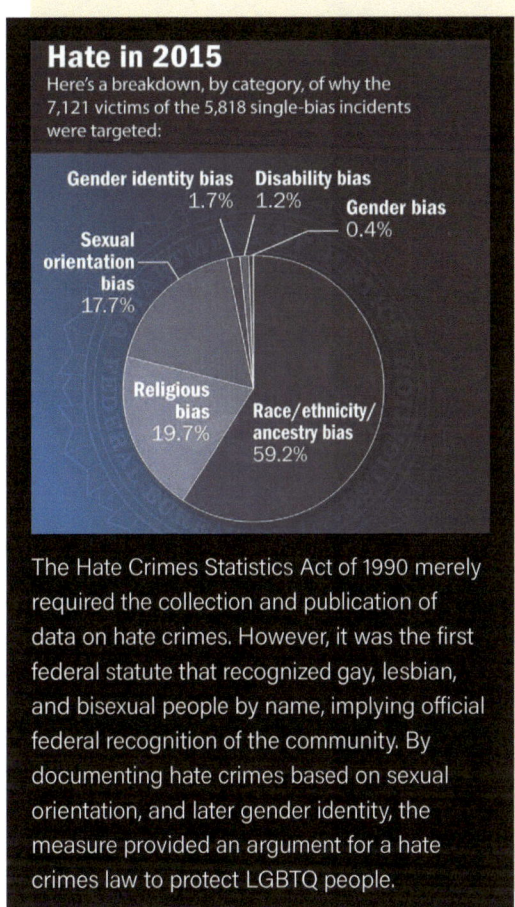

The Hate Crimes Statistics Act of 1990 merely required the collection and publication of data on hate crimes. However, it was the first federal statute that recognized gay, lesbian, and bisexual people by name, implying official federal recognition of the community. By documenting hate crimes based on sexual orientation, and later gender identity, the measure provided an argument for a hate crimes law to protect LGBTQ people.

DEFINITION OF TERMS

As the transgender community became more integrated into gay, lesbian, and bisexual community activism, the term LGBT (or GLBT) became common in the 1990s, while LGBTQ (lesbian, gay, bisexual, transgender, and queer) gained popularly in the 2000s. Alternative acronyms such as LGBTQIA (adding intersex and asexual), LGBTTQQIAAP (adding transsexual, questioning, ally, and pansexual), and other acronym combinations also proliferated in the 2000s. Queer gained increasing usage across this era as a positive all-inclusive umbrella term. Queer studies became an entrenched field in academia for the study and scholarship of gender and sexual identity.

MILITARY SERVICE

THE MILITARY BAN ON GAY AND lesbian people first gained national attention in 1975 with *Time* magazine's cover story on discharged Air Force Sergeant Leonard Matlovich, the magazine's first cover story of an openly LGBTQ person. Challenges to the ban on military service con-

Leonard Matlovich's tombstone at the Congressional Cemetery in Washington, D.C.

tinued through the 1980s and 1990s with prominent cases such as Miriam Ben-Shalom's fourteen-year court battle with the military, and Army Colonel Margarethe Cammermeyer successful challenge of her dismissal after 25 years of service.

In 1982, the military implemented Directive 1332.14, which changed homosexuality from a possible disqualification for military service to a mandatory one. Democratic presidential candidate Bill Clinton promised to overturn the military ban; however, when elected, he signed a compromise "Don't Ask, Don't Tell" (DADT) policy that allowed gay and lesbian people to serve in the military as long as they didn't come out publicly. Although the policy was intended to allow greater participation of gay and lesbian people in the military, the discharges continued at a high rate.

Through a combination of legal challenges, political pressure, and publicity, groups supporting LGBTQ service members were able to introduce a bill to Congress in 2006 to repeal DADT. Under pressure from a federal court decision that DADT was unconstitutional, a federal repeal of DADT was signed into law in 2010. However, the military continued upholding DADT policies until 2011 when a federal court finally ordered it to cease.

DISCRIMINATION

UNITED STATES HOUSE REPRESENTATIVE Bella Abzug introduced to Congress the Equality Act of 1974, the first federal civil rights act to include protection for gay and lesbian people. It failed. Gay and lesbian anti-discrimination bills were reintroduced through the 1970s, 1980s, and early 1990s, and although each garnered increasing support, it was never enough for passage. In 1996, the Employment Non-Discrimination Act (ENDA) was introduced to the floor of the United States Senate, but was defeated by a single vote. As of 2020, ENDA has yet to garner passage.

Executive orders were an easier method to extend LGBTQ protections. In 1998, President Clinton signed an executive order to prohibit discrimination based on sexual orientation in the federal service workforce. In 2014, President Obama signed an executive order to prohibit discrimination based on sexual orientation or gender identity for all federal contractors.

When the United States Supreme Court decided in 1986 that private sexual acts would continue to be deemed illegal in *Bowers v. Hardwick*, it threatened LGBTQ civil rights at a fundamental level. Many lower courts used the precedent to rule that LGBTQ people could be judged implicitly criminal and unfit for a number of rights. One example was the 1995 Virginia Supreme Court decision *Bottoms v. Bottoms*, in which Pamela Kay Bottoms won custody of her daughter Sharon's child in part because Sharon was openly lesbian. Following similar rationales, state supreme courts in North Carolina and Alabama affirmed the removal of children from lesbian and gay parents.

LGBTQ activists and organizations fought off discriminatory state initiatives in Idaho, Oregon and Maine in the mid-1990s. However in Colorado, they were not so successful. In reaction to lesbian and gay anti-discrimination ordinances adopted in Aspen, Boulder, and Denver, Colorado voters passed Amendment 2 in 1992 to prohibit any city, town, or county in the state from any action designed to protect its lesbian or gay citizens. LGBTQ activists fought the measure in the courts, and turned one of their biggest defeats into one of their biggest legal victories. In 1996, the United States Supreme Court ruled in *Romer v. Evans* that Colorado's Amendment 2 was unconstitutional. This Supreme Court decision was the first to claim that lesbian and gay people were equal to any other citizens and could not be denied participation in society and politics. Besides providing a legal standing to challenge government discrimination, it checked the power of voters or legislators to deny equal rights to LGBTQ people nationwide.

In 2003, the United States Supreme Court delivered another victory for LGBTQ rights when it ruled in *Lawrence v. Texas* that sodomy laws were unconstitutional. Just as the federal affirmation of sodomy laws had a wide-reaching impact on the LGBTQ community, so too did the abolition. When, in 2004, Massachusetts' judges ruled that the ban against same-sex marriage was unconstitutional, they cited *Lawrence v. Texas* and its implication that governments should not intrude on "consensual adult expressions of intimacy and one's choice of partner." *Lawrence v. Texas* also cast doubt on such far-reaching practices as the deportation of non-citizen same-sex partners of American citizens, the ban of LGBTQ people from military service, and the removal of children from LGBTQ parents.

Although *Romer v. Evans* and *Lawrence v. Texas* were critical decisions in supporting LGBTQ rights, the United States Supreme Court did not indicate by their rulings that LGBTQ citizens necessarily had the same status and rights as other minority groups. The justices ruled in 1995 that an LGBTQ group could legally be excluded from a public parade solely because parade organizers disapproved of their message. In 2000, the judges ruled that the Boy Scouts of America, as a private club, could exclude LGBTQ people because the latter's presence conflicted with the group's mission and beliefs. At at time when no gender, ethnic, or racial group could be excluded merely because an organization disapproved of them, these Supreme Court decisions suggested that LGBTQ people did not merit the same equal protection.

MARRIAGE

SAME-SEX MARRIAGE WAS FIRST publicized in an August 1953 cover story in *ONE Magazine*. That story resulted in the confiscation of the issue by postal authorities, who deemed the topic of same-sex marriage as a violation of obscenity statutes. In the gay liberation movement of the early 1970s, several same-sex couples applied for marriage licenses, but were universally denied. Legal challenges were similarly defeated.

The prohibition of gay and lesbian people from marriage had ramifications beyond the institution itself. It meant that same-sex partners of hospitalized LGBTQ people could be denied visitation and decision-making power. The death of an LGBTQ person left the surviving partner without any of the benefits granted to married couples. Lengthy legal battles were often required to recognize the survivor's rights in housing, inheritance, and child custody. Same-sex partners were barred from tax and insurance benefits. American citizens could not keep non-citizen same-sex partners from being

Although marriage permits could not be issued for same-sex marriages, couples still underwent marriage ceremonies across the country to affirm their commitment and love for one another. These marriage ceremonies took place (clockwise from upper left) in San Francisco (1973), Los Angeles, CA (1970); Jackson, MS (1989); and Philadelphia, PA (1957).

In 1974, Anthony Sullivan (right), an Australian citizen, had exhausted his legal options for remaining in the United States. When Sullivan and his partner Richard Adams, an American citizen, were refused legal recognition for their marriage, the Immigration and Naturalization Service initiated deportation proceedings. Refusing to end their fifteen year relationship, Sullivan and Adams went into hiding. They remained together in the United States until Adams' death in 2012.

deported. Same-sex partners could be excluded from adopting. LGBTQ status could be used to dismiss the custody claims of separated gay or lesbian parents.

In 1996, the Hawaii State Supreme Court ruled that the state could not legally deny same-sex couples the opportunity to marry. Although Hawaiian voters approved an amendment prohibiting the implementation of same-sex marriage, the court's decision ignited a backlash across the nation. By the end of 1996, sixteen states had implemented laws banning same-sex marriage, and the federal government had passed the Defense of Marriage Act (DOMA). DOMA denied same-sex couples the federal benefits and rights of marriage, even if a state legally recognized the union.

In 2000, Vermont passed the nation's first civil unions law, which conferred upon same-sex couples all the state's rights and benefits of married heterosexual couples. In 2004, the Massachusetts State Supreme Court ruled that the prohibition of same-sex marriage was unconstitutional, and the state became the first to officially recognize gay and lesbian marriages. In reaction, twenty-two more states instituted legislation banning same-sex marriage. An amendment to the United States constitution to ban same-sex marriage was proposed but defeated in 2004 and 2006.

Between 2004 and 2012, only six more states legalized same-sex marriage. Then from November 2012 to December 2013, 11 more states legalized same-sex marriage, bringing the total to 18. When Thea Spyer died in 2009, Edith "Edie" Windsor, her partner of over 40 years, was denied the federal estate tax exemption for surviving spouses because of DOMA and was sent a tax bill for $363,053. She sued, and in 2013, the United States Supreme Court ruled in *United States v. Windsor* that DOMA was unconstitutional, thereby granting same-sex married couples the same federal rights as heterosexual couples.

By 2015, multiple challenges to state bans on same-sex marriage had made their way through the court of appeals, with four rulings against the ban, and one upholding the ban. Consolidating the cases under *Obergefell v. Hodges*, the Supreme Court ruled that the Fourteenth Amendment to the United States Constitution gave same-sex couples the right to marry across the United States. The ruling overturned all state bans on same-sex marriage and granted all gay and lesbian United States citizens the right to marry regardless of where they lived.

The White House in rainbow colors to celebrate the Supreme Court decision on same-sex marriage.

PERSONAL STORY

LGBT Rights Movement

> **"I only have six months to live. I am sad, angry, and scared, but more than any of these things, I am grateful...to live for at least a short time as Michael, the man I was born to be."**

"I hereby grant your petition for a change of name and gender." With these five words by the judge, my life-long dream was realized; I was **officially male**! Growing up, I was told I was a girl and that no matter how much I wanted it, I would never be the boy that I wanted to be. At school, I was teased by classmates, and by the age of five, I had learned to be ashamed of who I was. At eleven, I started to develop breasts, the hideous **foreign objects** that tormented me every moment of every day. My attempts to hide them proved futile and I could not have been more disgusted and ashamed of my body.

I came out as a lesbian at nineteen, before coming out as transgender at thirty-two. Telling people you're a transman takes a whole different type of courage. While I ached for the love and support of my family, it was not to be. The good news is that the LGBTQ community embraced me, creating a new and more meaningful family of queer kinships.

Like most trans-identified men, I was socialized to adhere to female gender norms. Thus after coming out, I was constantly questioning my gender expression. Am I trans enough? Am I enough of a man? What makes a man a man? But I learned that I am a man simply because I say I am and I get to choose how to express my gender. Like sexuality, gender identity is fluid. It constantly evolves and each of us must find his or her **authentic self** in a hodgepodge of deeply ingrained stereotypes and expectations.

On August 13, 2014, I was told that due to brain cancer, I only have six months to live. I am sad, angry, and scared, but more than any of these things, I am **grateful**. I am grateful that my dream came true and that I had the opportunity to live for at least a short time as Michael, the man I was born to be.

– Michael Saum

TRANSGENDER EQUAL RIGHTS

ALTHOUGH THE 1980S SAW THE emergence of Lou Sullivan's FTM (female-to-male) International and Myrissa Sherrill Lynn's International Foundation for Gender Education, a national movement did not coalesce until the early years of the 1990s. The first Southern Comfort transgender conference began in 1991 and soon became one of the largest transgender gatherings in the country. Future Texas Judge, Phillis Frye, organized the first of six annual transgender law conferences the next year and also helped organize local transgender activists into a national contingent at the 1993 March on Washington. Fantasia Fair, a week-long conference for heterosexual MTF (male-to-female) cross-dressers that started in 1975, blossomed in the 1990s into a world renowned event for all transgender people.

ANDREA JENKINS
1961 –

Andrea Jenkins was the first openly transgender black woman elected in the United States, when she took office in the Minneapolis City Council in 2018. As of 2020, she served as vice president of the council and as chair of the Race Equity Subcommittee. In her previous work as a policy aide, curator, and artist, she long advocated on behalf of transgender voices.

KIM COCO IWAMOTO
1968 –

Kim Coco Iwamoto became the highest-ranked openly transgender official in the United States when she won a seat on Hawaii's Board of Education in 2006. Iwamoto has continuously advocated and worked with LGBTQ youth as a licensed therapeutic foster parent, lawyer and public figure. She was appointed to the Hawaii Civil Rights Commission in 2012.

Historically, murders of transgender people have been under-investigated, under-convicted, and under-punished. For example, when pioneering transgender activist Marsha P. Johnson was found floating in the Hudson River in 1992, the suspicious death was ruled a suicide with minimal investigation. When police refused to arrest transgender Brandon Teena's rapists in 1993, the rapists later hunted down and murdered Teena.

Legal and police practices regarding transgender victims has gradually improved. After the killers of Gwen Araujo tried to use a trans panic defense in 2004, California enacted legislation restricting the use of the victim-blaming tactic. The killer of Angie Zapata, murdered in Colorado in 2008, was the first to be convicted of a hate crime against a transgender person. A year later, Lateisha Green's murderer was convicted of a hate crime in New York.

Hate crimes and murders still disproportionately affect the transgender community. The brutal 1998 murder of Rita Hester led to a candlelight vigil in her honor and inspired Gwendolyn Ann Smith to start the Transgender Day of Remembrance the next year. The Day of Remembrance has since become an annual worldwide event held on November 20 to honor and raise awareness of those who die from transgender hate crimes every year.

Anne Ogborn created Transgender Nation within the San Francisco chapter of Queer Nation in 1992, with other chapters soon opening across the United States. Transgender Nation introduced a confrontational style of advocacy that had not been seen since Sylvia Rivera and Angela Davis in the 1970s. Riki Wilchens used this kind of activism in 1994 with her group Transexual Menace, which conducted vigils at court houses where transgender hate crime perpetrators were being tried.

Transgender issues had been historically neglected by mainstream gay and lesbian advocacy organizations. Gay and lesbian anti-discrimination measures often did not include protections for transgender people. However, transgender activists during this era increasingly integrated transgender issues into a broader LGBTQ movement. Although transgender people were unmentioned in previous Washington, D.C., marches, the 2000 Millennium March on Washington was the first to include a transgender plank. This more cohesive LGBTQ advocacy, combined with the emergence of local and national transgender advocacy groups, has had the power to affect greater political and social influence.

Minneapolis implemented the first municipal law protecting transgender citizens in 1976, with Harrisburg, Pennsylvania, and Seattle, Washington, following in the 1980s. By 2018, over 200 cities and counties had enacted laws protecting transgender people. Minnesota passed the first statewide protection for transgender people in 1993, and by 2018, had been joined by eighteen states and the District of Columbia.

In 2012, the federal government released a statement that transgender students are protected from discrimination under the provisions of Title IX, a federal law that prohibits sex discrimination in schools. The United States Department of Education issued guidelines for Title IX protection in 2014, a position later supported by the Justice Department. In 2013, California passed a law to require that public schools recognize a student's gender identity and to provide access to facilities based on that gender identification. The law was the first to specifically protect the rights of transgender students.

The mismatch of personal identity and official documentation creates huge challenges for those who have transitioned their gender identity. In 2010, the federal government changed their polity to allow gender changes on passports without requiring sex reassignment surgery. As of 2019, some states permit gender changes in state identity documents, others allow the change but only with proof of sex reassignment surgery, while two other states do not permit gender changes in state documentation. In 2017, Oregon became the first state to allow non-binary "X" gender markers on state identification documents, a move quickly followed by nineteen other states.

EPILOGUE

BATTLEFRONTS

[RELIGIOUS FREEDOM

TRANSGENDER
EQUAL RIGHTS

VISIBILITY]

RELIGIOUS FREEDOM

THE RELIGIOUS FREEDOM Restoration Act was signed into federal law in 1993 to protect diverse religious freedoms from government intrusion. By 2014, states had started introducing similar laws in an attempt to curtail freedoms provided to gay and lesbian people through federal recognition of same-sex marriages. In 2014, the Arizona legislature passed a religious freedom bill that was ultimately vetoed amid a wave of protest.

From 2015 to 2017, over 20 state legislatures introduced religious freedom bills. Two states passed religious freedom bills that permitted discrimination against gay and lesbian couples in fostering or adopting children, while two others addressed religious freedom in schools and counseling. Mississippi and Indiana passed broader versions of the bill, but Indiana, in reaction to protests, added an amendment protecting LGBTQ people from discrimination. In 2019, Texas passed SB1978 which protects companies that donate to anti-LGBTQ groups from any adverse action from the state government.

TRANSGENDER EQUAL RIGHTS

IN 2015, THE OBAMA administration, supported by a pentagon-commission study, lifted a ban on transgender people from serving in the armed forces. In 2017, President Trump issued a series of tweets to reinstate that ban, but lawsuits brought against the administration denied the re-implementation of the ban and allowed transgender people to enlist. However, by 2019, the Department of Defense had implemented policies to effectively restrict transgender service members from enlisting or serving in the military.

From 2015 to 2017, multiple states introduced bills to restrict male or female bathroom choice to the sex identified on a person's birth certificates. In 2016, North Carolina became the first state to pass such a bill, although the next year, the state repealed the portion of the bill relating to choice of bathrooms. As multiple states continued to debate bathroom bills in 2017, the Justice Department and Education department rescinded Department of Education and Justice Department guidances that transgender students were protected by Title IX, a statue that protects against sex discrimination.

Following a trend in court cases protecting transgender employees against discrimination, the Equal Employment Opportunity Commission ruled in *Macy v. Holder* that Title VII of the 1964 Civil Rights Act protected transgender employees from discrimination. The Department of Justice followed suit in 2014, supporting Title VII in application to gender identity discrimination claims. However, in

Epilogue

2017, the Department of Justice reversed their stance on Title VII and gender identity protection. In 2017, 2018 and 2019, the Department of Justice filed briefs to the United States Supreme Court that federal law does not prohibit discrimination against transgender people. Federal departments such as the Departments of Housing and Urban Development, Labor, Health and Human Services, and Education have each done away with protections for transgender people.

In 2020, the United States Supreme Court ruled in *Bostock v. Clayton County, Georgia* that Title VII of the Civil Rights Act of 1964 protects LGBTQ employees against discrimination. The court decided that the Title VII prohibition against discrimination based on sex included discrimination based on sexual orientation and gender identity, and that henceforth it would be illegal to fire someone on that basis. At the time of the decision, the majority of states had no law prohibiting the firing of a LGBTQ employee because of their sexual orientation or gender identity.

As of 2018, 28 states and the District of Columbia had enacted protections for transgender people. By 2017, 111 cities offered employee healthcare plans that explicitly covered transgender-related healthcare services. In a rare setback in 2015, Houston voters repealed the Houston Equal Rights Ordinance,

Protest against the proposed transgender military ban, 2017.

which protected LGBTQ people from discrimination, in part because it included protections for transgender people to choose the bathroom of their choice. Nonetheless by the end of 2016, over 225 cities and counties had enacted laws prohibiting discrimination on the basis of gender identity.

VISIBILITY

IN CITIES AND TOWNS ACROSS the world, yearly LGBTQ pride parades and festivals draw millions of participants. The parades and festivals benefit from extensive corporate sponsorship and the support of politicians and celebrities. March on Washington events in 1979, 1987, 1993, 2000, and 2009 collectively drew nearly two million participants. Unlike the media blackout of the 1979 and 1987 marches, each subsequent march has received national media coverage.

National Coming Out Day, established for LGBTQ people to declare their sexual orientation or gender identity, is celebrated on October 11 within LGBTQ history month. The day honors the empowerment of coming out to yourself, family, friends, and co-workers, and promotes the simple truth that people are more likely to support equality if they know someone who is LGBTQ. World AIDS Day, first held in 1988 to unite the fight against HIV and commemorate those who have died, is honored in hundreds of events around the world.

As of 2013, more than 500 openly LGBTQ people served at all levels of government. In 2016, Oregon elected Kate Brown as the nation's first openly gay governor; and in 2017, Virginia elected Danica Roem as the nation's first openly transgender state representative. In 2019, Pete Buttigieg became the

Queer-identified Alicia Garza (left) and Patrisse Cullors (center) joined with Opal Tometi to found Black Lives Matters (BLM) in 2013. In 2020, BLM led up to 15,000 people in a rally in New York to support Black transgender people, one of the largest transgender rights protests in history. In 2013, transgender woman Elle Hearns (inset photo) co-founded the Black Lives Matter Global Network. She also founded and served as executive director of the Martha P. Johnson Institute, which protects and defends the human rights of Black transgender people.

Epilogue

most visible LGBTQ person to seek the presidential nomination. The economic clout and organizational skills of the LGBTQ community have worked to discourage discriminatory policies aimed at LGBTQ employees, patrons, and students. Most large companies today have anti-discrimination policies and provide equal benefits to all employees.

In 2011, The Williams Institute, a national LGBTQ think tank, estimated that roughly 9 million Americans identify as LGBTQ. They occupy every aspect of life, are visible in every culture and society, and can trace their history to the beginnings of human civilization. As religious freedom bills and discriminatory transgender policies demonstrate, full equality has yet to be achieved. Discrimination and hate crimes continue to proliferate. However as of 2020, the LGBTQ community has never been as well-positioned to meet those challenges and to seek equality for all in the community. As the militant activist group Queer Nation said in their famous rallying cry: "We're here. We're queer. Get used to it."

The great diversity of the LGBTQ community comes to full display at yearly gay pride parades.

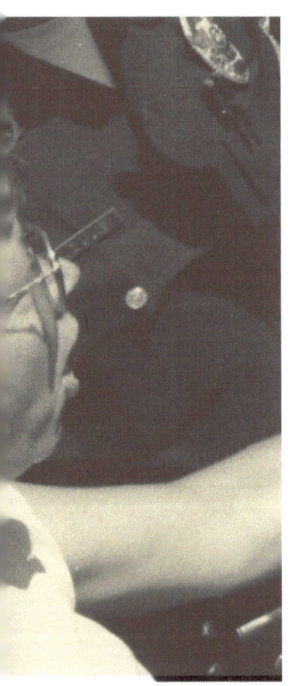
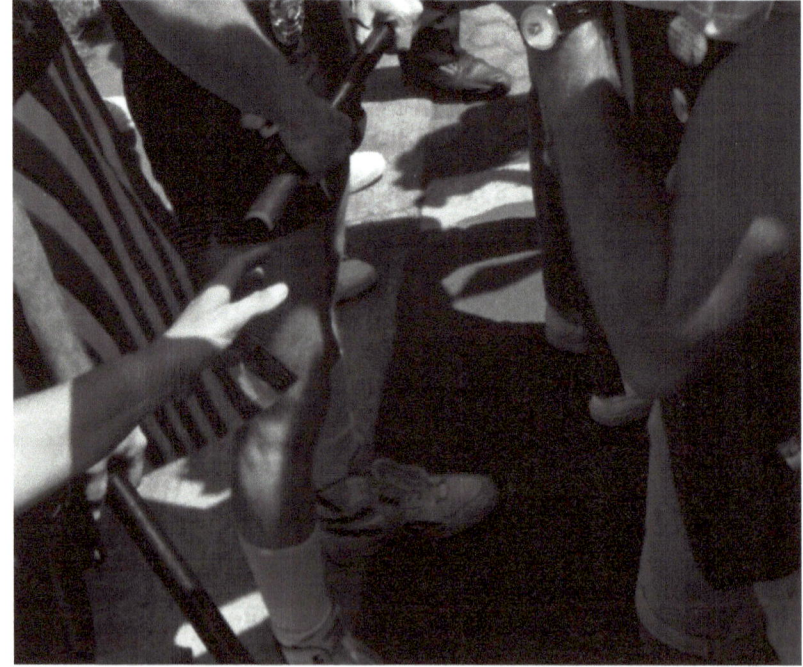

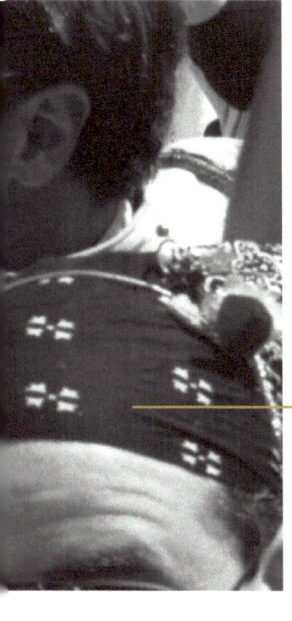

APPENDICES

TEN ORGANIZATIONS
TO KNOW

TEN TEXTS TO KNOW

TEN HISTORY BOOKS
TO KNOW

TEN COURT CASES
TO KNOW

GLOSSARY

PHOTO CREDITS

BIBLIOGRAPHY

TEN ORGANIZATIONS TO KNOW

GAY & LESBIAN ALLIANCE AGAINST DEFAMATION

The Gay and Lesbian Alliance Against Defamation formed in New York City in 1985 to protest the New York Post's sensationalized AIDS news coverage. Over the years, GLAAD expanded to become a national watchdog and advocacy group to combat prejudicial LGBTQ coverage in the media, whether on printed material, radio, television, film, or the internet. To combat the use of pejoratives when referring to LGBTQ people, GLAAD compiled a Media Reference Guide to provide media outlets with neutral terms in place of offensive ones. GLAAD's Media Awards have been a fixture since 1989, recognizing fair and inclusive media representations of the LGBTQ community.

GAY, LESBIAN & STRAIGHT EDUCATION NETWORK

Founded by Kevin Jennings in Massachusetts in 1990, GLSEN aims to reform the United States educational system by ensuring a safe environment for K-12 students. Its first victory was in 1993, when its home state became the first to prohibit discrimination against LGBTQ public school students. The organization went national two years later and, as of 2019, has 43 local chapters. It has registered over 4,000 Gay Straight Alliances in schools throughout the country and offers resources to student clubs, lesson plans to instructors, and training techniques to administrators.

HUMAN RIGHTS CAMPAIGN

Committed to mainstream political advocacy and organizing, the Human Rights Campaign is the largest LGBTQ advocacy group in the nation. Formed partly in response to the rise of the conservative movement in the late 1970s, its first director, Steve Endean, saw a need to expand beyond state and local politics to national-level organizing. HRC works within existing structures to make heard its voice in elections, lobbying, and policy reform. Its annual "Corporate Equality Index" reports on the practices of leading companies in regards to their treatment of LGBTQ employees. In 2015, HRC claimed a whopping 1.5 million members.

INTERSEX SOCIETY OF NORTH AMERICA

For much of the 20th century, doctors would surgically assign gender to babies born with ambiguous genitalia, often without the parent's knowledge. Cheryl Chase founded the Intersex Society of North America in 1993 to "end the shame, secrecy, and unwanted genital surgeries" for intersex people. ISNA has led to improved medical decisions as well as greater visibility to intersex people and increased scholarship on intersex issues.

LAMBDA LEGAL DEFENSE AND EDUCATION FUND

Formed by volunteers in 1973, the nation's largest public-interest law firm for the rights of LGBTQ persons was at first refused the right to exist by authorities in New York State who denied that furthering gay rights was a "charitable or benevolent" purpose. Short on funds in its early years, Lambda Legal worked as a "friend of the court" in New York before securing enough money to go national. Lambda Legal works on the local, state and federal levels and has been a part of the some of the most important LGBTQ judicial decisions such as the United States Supreme Court cases *Romer v. Evans* and *Lawrence v. Texas*.

NATIONAL GAY AND LESBIAN TASK FORCE

Formed in 1973, the NGLTF grew out of the New York-based Gay Activists Alliance to become the first national LGBTQ advocacy group. In the 1970s, NGLTF helped end the federal ban on gay and lesbian employees, advocated for the first congressional gay and lesbian anti-discrimination bill, and helped arrange the first gay and lesbian meeting at the White House. In the 1980s, NGLTF helped overturn an Oklahoma law prohibiting teachers from speaking positively about anything gay or lesbian, initiated the era's most significant LGBTQ anti-violence project, and mobilized the earliest campaign for a federal response to the AIDS crisis. Today, the NGLTF continues to fight for LGBTQ civil rights and equality by supporting the grassroots power of LGBTQ communities.

PARENTS, FAMILIES AND FRIENDS OF LESBIANS AND GAYS

After the vicious beating of Gay Activists Alliance members and the refusal of police to intervene, Jeanne Manford marched in New York's 1972 pride parade with a sign supportive of her gay son. Noting the emotional response it evoked, she determined to create a support group dedicated to bridging the gaps in understanding between heterosexual parents and their LGBTQ children. As of 2019, PFLAG's more than 400 chapters and 200,000 supporters lobby for policies supporting LGBTQ people, including workplace equality, safe and welcoming schools, transgender rights, and ending reparative therapy practices.

SERVICEMEMBERS LEGAL DEFENSE FUND

SLDN formed in 1993 to support LGBTQ armed forces personnel in the wake of the "Don't Ask, Don't Tell" (DADT) policy. It brought to light the murder of soldier Barry Winchell after months of bullying. Ten years later, SLDN supported combat veteran Dan Choi when he effectively ended his career by coming out on national television. The organization helped introduce the first bill to repeal DADT to Congress in 2006, and helped support its passage in 2010.

TRANSGENDER LAW CENTER

TLC formed in 2002 to work for those discriminated against because of their gender identity or expression. TLC has worked on law, policy, and attitudes around transgender issues of legal name changes, immigration, AIDS services and prevention, safe access to restrooms, education, bullying, health care, marriage equality, treatment of prisoners, political advocacy, economic empowerment, and discrimination. It has helped facilitate municipal, state, and federal laws to protect transgender people and provided educational workshops to the public and the legal community regarding transgender law and issues.

VICTORY FUND

Inspired by the success of the women's donor network EMILY's List, the Victory Fund formed to assist openly LGBTQ politicians gain office. In 1991, their efforts led to the election in Seattle of Sherry Harris, the nation's first openly lesbian African-American city council member. Since then, it has supported thousands of openly LGBTQ elected officials who serve in all levels of government, and who have advanced LGBTQ rights across the country.

TEN TEXTS TO KNOW

MATTACHINE SOCIETY STATEMENT OF PURPOSE AND MEMBERSHIP PLEDGE
HARRY HAY (1951)

Formed in Los Angeles in 1951, the Mattachine Society was one of the earliest LGBTQ organizations in the U.S. Their aim was to have discussion groups and grow a cohesive identity and minority consciousness.

> *While there are undoubtedly individual homosexuals who number many of their own people among their friends, thousands of homosexuals live out their lives bewildered, unhappy, alone— isolated from their own kind and unable to adjust to the dominant culture. Even those who may have many homosexual friends are still cut off from the deep satisfactions man's gregarious nature can achieve only when he is consciously part of a larger unified whole. A major purpose of the Mattachine Society is to provide a consensus of principle around which all of our people can rally and from which they can derive a feeling of belonging.*

A GAY MANIFESTO
CARL WITTMAN (1969–1970)

Wittman's commitment to social justice, honed during his work with Students for a Democratic Society, led to a radical vision for gay liberation coupled with a more general sexual liberation agenda for all.

> *Conclusion: An Outline of Imperatives for Gay Liberation*
>
> 1. *Free ourselves: come out everywhere; initiate self defense and political activity; initiate counter community institutions.*
> 2. *Turn other gay people on: talk all the time; understand; forgive, accept.*
> 3. *Free the homosexual in everyone… be gentle, and keep talking and acting free.*
> 4. *We've been playing an act for a long time, so we're consummate actors. Now we can begin to be, and it'll be a good show!*

THE WOMAN-IDENTIFIED WOMAN
RADICALESBIANS (1970)

Second-wave feminism was initially hostile to lesbians. At the Second Congress to Unite Women, a group calling itself Radicalesbians distributed a flyer demanding a discussion of lesbianism in the women's movement.

> *It is the primacy of women relating to women, of women creating a new consciousness of and with each other which is at the heart of the women's liberation, and the basis for the cultural revolution. Together we must find, reinforce and validate our authentic selves. As we do this, we confirm in each other that struggling incipient sense of pride and strength, the divisive barriers begin to melt, we feel this growing solidarity with our sisters. We see ourselves as prime, find our centers inside of ourselves. We find receding the sense of alienation, of being cut off, of being*

behind a locked window, of being unable to get out what we know is inside. We feel a realness, feel at last we are coinciding with ourselves. With that real self, with that consciousness, we begin a revolution to end the imposition of all coercive identifications, and to achieve maximum autonomy in human expression.

THE OPPRESSED SHALL NOT BECOME THE OPPRESSOR
THE THIRD WORLD GAY REVOLUTION (1970)

Black and Latino gay men came together in 1970 to form The Third World Gay Revolution. Written in English and Spanish, this manifesto speaks out against the oppression of gay people of color within their own communities.

> *Sisters and Brothers of the Third World, you who call yourselves "revolutionaries" have failed to deal with your sexist attitudes. Instead you cling to male-supremacy and therefore to the conditioned role of oppressors. Brothers still fight for the privileged position of man-on-the-top. Sisters quickly fall in line behind-their-men. By your counterrevolutionary struggle to maintain and to force heterosexuality and the nuclear family, you perpetuate outmoded remnants of Capitalism. By your anti-homosexual stance you have used the weapons of the oppressor thereby becoming the agent of the oppressor.*

NOW RESOLUTION
NATIONAL ORGANIZATION FOR WOMEN (1971)

Less than one year after the purge of lesbian members from NOW, this formal resolution won approval at the NOW national convention and brought lesbians and lesbian issues permanently into the feminist movement.

> *THEREFORE, BE IT RESOLVED: That NOW recognizes the double oppression of women who are lesbians, and*
>
> *BE IT FURTHER RESOLVED: That a woman's right to her own person includes the right to define and express her own sexuality and to choose her own lifestyle, and*
>
> *BE IT FURTHER RESOLVED: That NOW acknowledge the oppression of lesbians as a legitimate concern of feminism.*

A BLACK FEMINIST STATEMENT
COMBAHEE RIVER COLLECTIVE (1977)

Belonging to the Civil Rights and women's movement's, but not fully represented in either, the Massachusetts-based Combahee River Collective articulated the black feminist lesbian perspective. This was an entirely new viewpoint and had to be created, a member said, from scratch.

> *We believe that sexual politics under patriarchy is as pervasive in Black women's lives as are the politics of class and race. We also often find it difficult to separate race from class from sex oppression because in our lives they are most often experienced*

simultaneously. We know that there is such a thing as racial-sexual oppression which is neither solely racial nor solely sexual, e.g., the history of rape of Black women by white men as a weapon of political repression.

Although we are feminists and Lesbians, we feel solidarity with progressive Black men and do not advocate the fractionalization that white women who are separatists demand. Our situation as Black people necessitates that we have solidarity around the fact of race, which white women of course do not need to have with white men, unless it is their negative solidarity as racial oppressors. We struggle together with Black men against racism, while we also struggle with Black men about sexism."

THE DENVER PRINCIPLES
PEOPLE WITH AIDS (1983)

The Denver Principles were created at the founding meeting of the National Association of People with AIDS. The principles set the foundation of how people with AIDS should be regarded and treated… primarily as people first.

We condemn attempts to label us as "victims," which implies defeat, and we are only occasionally "patients," which implies passivity, helplessness, and dependence upon the care of others. We are "people with AIDS."

We recommend that all people:

Support us in our struggle against those who would fire us from our jobs, evict us from our homes, refuse to touch us, separate us from our loved ones, our community, or our peers, since there is no evidence that AIDS can be spread by casual social contact.

Do not scapegoat people with AIDS, blame us for the epidemic, or generalize about our lifestyles.

1,112 AND COUNTING
LARRY KRAMER (1983)

In 1983, the new epidemic AIDS had generated a largely tepid response within the gay community. Author and playwright Kramer, who had already helped found the Gay Men's Health Crisis, here used analysis and rhetoric to mobilize his community to political action in the pages of the *New York Native*.

I am angry and frustrated almost beyond the bound my skin and bones and body and brain can encompass. My sleep is tormented by nightmares and visions of lost friends, and my days are flooded by the tears of funerals and memorial services and seeing my sick friends. How many of us must die before all of us living fight back?

I know that unless I fight with every ounce of my energy I will hate myself. I hope, I pray, I implore you to feel the same.

WHY A BLACK GAY CHURCH?
JAMES S. TINNEY (1986)

Minister, journalist, speechwriter, and professor, Tinney's passion for Black Pentecostalism and for political mobilization led to this article, which focuses on bridging gay liberation and worship.

> *White gay churches have, within the past 10 years or more, come into existence under circumstances related to the oppression of sexual identity that parallel the circumstances related to oppression of Black identity. Unfortunately, however, many Black lesbians and gays find the same racial oppressiveness in these white gay churches that Blacks generally experience in predominantly white churches of whatever label.*
>
> *Black gay churches should be supported because, on the one hand, they represent the pluralism that America and American Christianity are supposed to represent; and on the other hand, they represent the same desire for freedom, access, encouragement, understanding, and recognition that Blacks find impossible in most white churches, and that white gays find impossible in most "straight" churches.*

THE EMPIRE STRIKES BACK: A POSTRANSSEXUAL MANIFESTO
SANDY STONE (1988)

A new and emboldened transgender movement emerged in the late 1980s and early 1990s. This essay, first presented in 1988 and then published in 1991, participated in the redefinition of the movement and the beginning of transgender scholarship.

> *The essence of transsexualism is the act of passing... I could not ask a transsexual for anything more inconceivable than to forgo passing, to be consciously "read", to read oneself aloud--and by this troubling and productive reading, to begin to write oneself into the discourses by which one has been written--in effect, then, to become a [look out-- dare I say it again?] postranssexual. Still, transsexuals know that silence can be an extremely high price to pay for acceptance. I want to speak directly to the brothers and sisters who may read/"read" this and say: I ask all of us to use the strength which brought us through the effort of restructuring identity, and which has also helped us to live in silence and denial, for a re-visioning of our lives. I know you feel that most of the work is behind you and that the price of invisibility is not great. But, although individual change is the foundation of all things, it is not the end of all things. Perhaps it's time to begin laying the groundwork for the next transformation.*

TEN HISTORY BOOKS TO KNOW

EARLY 20ᵀᴴ

GAY NEW YORK: GENDER, URBAN CULTURE, AND THE MAKING OF THE GAY MALE WORLD
GEORGE CHAUNCEY (1994)

This study on homosexuality in early 20th century New York is one of the best non-fiction historical accounts on any topic.

> Chauncey, George. *Gay New York: Gender, Urban Culture, and the Making of the Gay Male World.* New York: BasicBooks, 1994.

1940s

COMING OUT UNDER FIRE: THE HISTORY OF GAY MEN AND WOMEN IN WORLD WAR TWO
ALLAN BÉRUBÉ (1990)

Bérubé explores the rich gay and lesbian experience during World War II.

> Bérubé, Allan. *Coming Out Under Fire: The History of Gay Men and Women in World War Two.* New York: Free Press, 1990.

1950s

SEXUAL POLITICS, SEXUAL COMMUNITIES: THE MAKING OF A HOMOSEXUAL MINORITY IN THE UNITED STATES, 1940 - 1970
JOHN D'EMILIO (1983)

This foundational work detailed the gay rights movement that preceded Stonewall. Read David Johnson's *Lavender Scare* and Craig Loftin's *Letters to ONE* for other must-read accounts of this era.

> D'Emilio, John. *Sexual Politics, Sexual Communities: the Making of a Homosexual Minority in the United States, 1940–1970.* Chicago: The University of Chicago Press, 1983.

1969

STONEWALL
DAVID CARTER (2004)

Carter's work is the most exhaustive account of this historic event. Also be sure to read famed LGBTQ chronicler Martin Duberman's coverage of the event and its context through the eyes of six diverse participants.

> Carter, David. *Stonewall.* New York: St. Martin's Press, 2004.

1970s

OUT FOR GOOD: THE STRUGGLE TO BUILD A GAY RIGHTS MOVEMENT
DUDLEY CLENDINEN & ADAM NAGOURNEY (1999)

While other books expertly detail this era from the context of specific cities, no book better captures the 1970s national gay rights movement.

> Clendinen, Dudley and Nagourney, Adam. *Out for Good: The Struggle to Build a Gay Rights Movement in America*. New York: Simon & Schuster, 1999.

1980s

AND THE BAND PLAYED ON: POLITICS, PEOPLE AND THE AIDS EPIDEMIC
RANDY SHILTS (1987)

Randy Shilts' three books are the gold standard of gay and lesbian journalistic non-fiction. *And the Band Played On* is required reading to the most devastating era in American gay history.

> Shilts, Randy. *And the Band Played on: Politics, People and the AIDS Epidemic*. New York: St. Martin's Press, 1987.

LEGAL

FROM THE CLOSET TO THE COURTROOM: FIVE LGBT RIGHTS LAWSUITS THAT HAVE CHANGED OUR NATION
CARLOS A. BALL (2010)

Many great legal books could have been noted here, but this book is a focused account of five lawsuits that should be covered in every American history class.

> Ball, Carlos A. *From the Closet to the Courtroom: Five LGBT Rights Lawsuits That Have Changed our Nation*. Boston: Beacon Press, 2010.

LESBIAN

ODD GIRLS AND TWILIGHT LOVERS: A HISTORY OF LESBIAN LIFE IN TWENTIETH-CENTURY AMERICA
LILLIAN FADERMAN (1991)

This is the foundational account of lesbian life in 20th century America. For an additional treat, try Faderman's *Gay Revolution*, one of the best comprehensive histories of the gay rights movement.

> Faderman, Lillian. *Odd Girls and Twilight Lovers: A History of Lesbian Life in Twentieth-Century America.* New York: Columbia University Press, 1991.

MEDIA

THE CELLULOID CLOSET: HOMOSEXUALITY IN THE MOVIES
VITO RUSSO (1987)

Russo's seminal research gave rise to the study of homosexuality in media.

> Russo, Vito. *The Celluloid Closet: Homosexuality in the Movies.* Revised edition. New York: Harper and Row, Publishers, 1987.

TRANSGENDER

HOW SEX CHANGED: A HISTORY OF TRANSSEXUALITY IN THE UNITED STATES
JOANNE MEYEROWITZ (2002)

Susan Stryker's *Transgender History* is better known and an excellent account, but Joanne Meyerowitz's work taps the Kinsey Institute's treasured archives to great effect.

> Meyerowitz, Joanne. *How Sex Changed: A History of Transsexuality in the United States.* Cambridge: Harvard University Press, 2002.

TEN COURT CASES TO KNOW

ONE, INC. V. OLESEN
SUPREME COURT OF THE UNITED STATES (1958)

ONE, Inc. v. Olesen was the first Supreme Court decision in favor of LGBTQ rights. Los Angeles Postmaster Olesen seized mailings of the early gay and lesbian movement's *ONE Magazine* on the basis that it promoted homosexuality and thus was inherently obscene. The Supreme Court reversed the lower court decisions and cleared the way for the broad circulation of LGBTQ publications.

BOUTILIER V. IMMIGRATION AND NATURALIZATION SERVICE
SUPREME COURT OF THE UNITED STATES (1967)

Boutilier v. Immigration and Naturalization Service affirmed the right of the INS to deny immigration to gay and lesbian people. The Immigration and Nationality Act of 1952 denied any people with a "psychopathic personality" from entering the United States, a designation that included LGBTQ people. When homosexuality was declassified as a mental illness in 1973, the INS continued to deny gay and lesbian people entry and to actively deport gay and lesbian immigrants until a change in policy in 1979.

NORTON V. MACY
UNITED STATES COURT OF APPEALS FOR THE DISTRICT OF COLUMBIA CIRCUIT (1969)

Norton v. Macy rejected the policy of the United State Civil Service Commission to disqualify applicants and terminate employees based on sexual orientation. Although previous court cases such as *Scott v. Macy* had challenged the exclusionary policy, this court case was the first to directly repudiate the Commission's policy. In 1975, the commission would finally drop is policy banning gay and lesbian people for employment.

BOWERS V. HARDWICK
SUPREME COURT OF THE UNITED STATES (1986)

Bowers v. Hardwick reversed a federal district court's finding that an anti-sodomy statute violated a LGBTQ person's fundamental right to privacy. Hardwick, arrested for alleged consensual sex with a man in his bedroom, was prosecuted for the crime of sodomy. Until this decision was reversed seventeen years later, it would allow for the continuing denial of a broad range of civil rights for LGBTQ people.

PRICE WATERHOUSE V. HOPKINS
SUPREME COURT OF THE UNITED STATES (1989)

Price Waterhouse v. Hopkins affirmed that the prohibition in the Civil Rights Act of 1964 against gender discrimination extended to discrimination based on gender-role stereotypes. Employee Ann Hopkins was rejected for promotion because she did not behave in a "feminine" manner. In finding for her, the court concluded that the Civil Rights Act barred not just discrimination based on the biological differences between women and men, but also discrimination based on a person's failure to conform to socially-constructed gender expectations.

ROMER V. EVANS
SUPREME COURT OF THE UNITED STATES (1996)

Romer v. Evans overturned Colorado's state constitutional Amendment 2, passed by voters, which prohibited any city, town, or county in the state from any action designed to protect gay and lesbian people. The court ruled that the amendment violated the rights of gay and lesbian citizens to participate in society and politics. Besides becoming a legal standing to challenge government discrimination, it checked the power of voters or legislators to deny equal rights to LGBTQ people.

LAWRENCE V. TEXAS
SUPREME COURT OF THE UNITED STATES (2003)

Lawrence v. Texas reversed the court's finding in 1986's *Bowers v. Hardwick* by invalidating a Texas sodomy law. The court found that "the liberty protected by the Constitution allows homosexual persons the right to choose to enter upon relationships in the confines of their homes and their own private lives and still retain their dignity as free persons." The decision would have a broad impact on the fight for LGBTQ civil rights, including on the denial of same-sex marriage, deportation of LGBTQ people, ban of LGBTQ people from military service, and removal of children from LGBTQ parents.

UNITED STATES V. WINDSOR
SUPREME COURT OF THE UNITED STATES (2013)

United States v. Windsor ruled that a section of the Defense of Marriage Act (DOMA) was unconstitutional and that the federal government could not discriminate against married lesbian and gay couples for the purposes of determining federal benefits and protections. The court held that the act was "unconstitutional as a deprivation of the equal liberty of persons that is protected by the Fifth Amendment."

OBERGEFELL V. HODGES
SUPREME COURT OF THE UNITED STATES (2015)

Obergefell v. Hodges gave same-sex couples the right to marry across the United States. At the time, each state set its own policy towards same-sex marriage, meaning married couples recognized in one state, may not be recognized in another. This case, a consolidation six separate cases into one, officially made same-sex marriage a right guaranteed by the United States Constitution.

BOSTOCK V. CLAYTON COUNTY, GEORGIA
SUPREME COURT OF THE UNITED STATES (2020)

Bostock v. Clayton County, Georgia ruled that LGBTQ people are protected from employment discrimination by Title VII of the Civil Rights Act of 1964, which prohibits discrimination based on race, color, religion, sex, and national origin. The court defined that discrimination based on sexual orientation and gender identity was, by its very definition, discrimination based on sex.

GLOSSARY

> Note that every term has generational, cultural and geographical specificities. This glossary is not an exhaustive list of the terms people use to describe their identities.

AIDS – acquired immunodeficiency syndrome, the result of an HIV infection and the collapse of the immune system.

Bisexual or bi – an individual who is physically, romantically and/or emotionally attracted to men and women. Bisexuals need not have had sexual experience with both men and women.

Cisgender – an individual whose gender expression and identity align with the gender the person was assigned at birth.

Civil unions – state-based legal recognition of non-heterosexual couples which offers some or all of the state's rights, protections, and responsibilities of marriage.

Closet – a metaphorical place in which to hide one's LGBTQ orientation.

Coming out – process of disclosing one's sexual orientation or gender identity to oneself, some, or all people.

Conversion or reparative therapy – formal attempt to change a person's gay or lesbian sexual orientation to heterosexual. Illegal in some states due to the danger to the individuals treated.

Cross-dresser – one who wears clothing typically associated with the gender of the opposite sex. Cross-dressing does not indicate sexual orientation or gender identity.

Disorderly conduct – a catch-all ordinance used against LGBTQ people to cite or arrest for any behavior judged as disruptive.

Drag – wearing clothing typically associated with a different gender, often for a performance in which gender is highlighted. Drag kings present themselves as male; drag queens present themselves as female. Drag does not indicate sexual orientation or gender identity.

Entrapment – police tactic in which a suspected gay man is approached for sex and, after agreeing, is arrested on a morals charge.

FTM – female-to-male transgender person.

Gay – term adopted in the early 20th century to denote those whose enduring physical, romantic, and/or emotional attractions are to people of the same sex. It has been used as an umbrella term for LGBTQ. Since the 1970s, "Lesbian" is a preferred term for women.

Gay-in – a gay version of the 1960s counter-cultural "love-ins," essentially outdoor festival-type parties.

Gay panic defense – a legal defense that exculpates the perpetrator of a violent crime against a gay or lesbian person if the gay or lesbian person is perceived to have made a sexual advance.

Gender expression – how one outwardly expresses one's gender identity, via clothing, hairstyles, behavior, etc.

Gender identity – how one places oneself along a continuum between male, female, and other. Gender identity does not necessarily accord with the gender one is at birth and is not always visible.

Gender identity disorder – a controversial diagnostic term [DSM-IV] given to transgender and other people who do not conform to expected gender norms in dress, play or behavior. Gender-variant people consider the term offensive as they are not "disordered."

Gender nonconformity – when gender expression or identity does not conform to societal stereotypes of male or female.

Genderqueer – a term denoting a person who considers one's own identity to be outside the binary male/female designations.

Heteronormativity – the assumption that heterosexuality is the sole acceptable sexual orientation.

Heterosexism – attitudes, bias and discrimination in favor of heterosexuality.

Heterosexual – a person whose enduring physical, romantic and/or emotional attractions are to those of the opposite sex.

HIV – human immunodeficiency virus, the virus that causes AIDS.

Homosexual – a person whose enduring physical, romantic, and/or emotional attractions are to those of the same sex. Currently considered out-fashioned or even offensive; "gay" or "lesbian" are preferred terms.

Homophile movement – mid-20th century social movement in which gay and lesbian people challenged discriminatory practices and attitudes.

Homophobia – an irrational fear of or aversion to LGBTQ people or to those perceived to be LGBTQ.

Internalized homophobia – accepting homophobic fears and aversion in regards to one's own LGBTQ identity.

Intersex – term describing a person whose biological sex is ambiguous. Intersex conditions can affect the genitals, chromosomes, or secondary sex characteristics.

Lavender menace – term of antipathy toward lesbians within the early days of second-wave feminism. First used by Betty Friedan to object to lesbians declaring themselves within the women's movement.

Lesbian – woman whose enduring physical, romantic, and/or emotional attractions are to other women.

Lewd conduct – a catch-all ordinance used against LGBTQ people to cite or arrest for any conduct judged to arouse the libido.

LGBT – Lesbian, Gay, Bisexual, and Transgender. This is an umbrella term.

MTF – male-to-female transgender person.

Morals charge – a citation or arrest for any sexual behavior judged to offend public morals.

Outing – the act of publicly declaring someone's sexual orientation or gender identity without that person's consent

Pansexual – an individual who is physically, romantically and/or emotionally attracted to people of all gender identities.

Patriarchy – a society organized around male privilege and power.

Queer – an umbrella term which includes all LGBT people and anyone who chooses to identify as such. This term is still considered pejorative by some and should be used with sensitivity.

Sex reassignment surgery – formerly known as a "sex change operation," this can be one step in transitioning from one gender identity to another.

Sexual orientation – an individual's physical, romantic, and/or emotional attraction to another person. This can be fluid and is not to be confused with gender identity.

Sodomy – a biblical term referring to anal intercourse, but broadly construed in the 20th century as any non-procreative sexual activity.

Trans panic defense – a legal defense that exculpates the perpetrator of a violent crime against a transgender person if the transgender person is perceived to have made a sexual advance or has engaged in sexual activity without previously disclosing their transgender identity.

Transgender – an umbrella term for people whose gender identity, expression, or behavior differs from those typically associated with the sex they were at birth.

Transition – process of altering one's birth sex.

Transsexual – older term for a person with a gender different from his or her birth sex. Generally not used today, transgender being the preferred term.

Two-spirit – an umbrella term for a Native American belief holding that there are several genders. Two-spirited people have more than a single gender within them.

Zap – a political action that utilizes surprise, personal confrontation, and theatrics to make a point.

Terms and basics of definitions were collated from the following sources: GLSEN, GLAAD, Revel and Riot, National Council of Teachers of English, and UC Davis' LGBT Center.

Appendices

PHOTO CREDITS

THE BEGINNINGS

p. 01 – Chapter Image
    ONE Incorporated Records, ONE Archives at the USC Libraries

p. 03 – Prison Bars
    Photograph by Pat Rocco, Pat Rocco Photographs and Papers, ONE Archives at the USC Libraries

p. 07 – Gertrude "Ma" Rainey
    Public Domain: https://en.wikipedia.org/wiki/Ma_Rainey

p. 07 – Gladys Bentley
    Public Domain: https://en.wikipedia.org/wiki/Gladys_Bentley

p. 08 – Dr. Harry Benjamin
    Kinsey Institute for Research in Sex, Gender, and Reproduction

p. 09 – Behavior Modification Kits
    ONE Subject Files Collection, ONE Archives at the USC Libraries

p. 10 – Women Working on Plane
    Esther Herbert and Marvyl Doyle Papers and Photographs, ONE Archives at the USC Libraries

p. 11 – Bayard Rustin
    Library of Congress Prints and Photographs division, digital ID ppmsc.01272

p. 12 – Pearl M. Hart
    Courtesy of Gerber/Hart Library and Archives

p. 13 – Henry Gerber
    Public Domain: https://en.wikipedia.org/wiki/Henry_Gerber

p. 14 – ONE Magazine Cover
    ONE Magazine, 9, no. 8 (August 1961): Cover. ONE Archives at the USC Libraries

p. 15 – *Sexual Behavior in the Human Male*
    Book library, ONE Archives at the USC Libraries

p. 16 – James Baldwin
    Distinguished Visiting Professor at Miami Dade College, Miami Dade College Archives

p. 17 – Assorted Images
    Blue Max Motorcycle Club Records (top left), ONE Archives Subject File Photographs (top right), ONE Incorporated Records (bottom), ONE Archives at the USC Libraries

THE HOMOPHILE MOVEMENT

p. 18 – Chapter Image
    Photograph by Kay Tobin Lahusen, Barbara Gittings and Kay Tobin Lahusen Gay History Papers and Photographs, New York Public Library

p. 21 – William Koelsch
    Courtesy of William Koelsch

p. 24 – *Homosexual in America*
    Book library, ONE Archives at the USC Libraries

p. 25 – José Julio Sarria
    Harold L. Call Papers, ONE Archives at the USC Libraries

p. 26 – Mattachine Society Members
    Harry Hay Papers, ONE Archives at the USC Libraries

p. 26 – Harry Hay
    Harry Hay Papers, ONE Archives at the USC Libraries

p. 27 – Slater, Legg, and Kepner
    ONE Incorporated Records, ONE Archives at the USC Libraries

p. 27 – Christine Jorgensen
    ONE Incorporated Records, ONE Archives at the USC Libraries

p. 28 – *Keval* Autograph Party
    ONE Incorporated Records, ONE Archives at the USC Libraries

p. 28 – Del Martin and Phyllis Lyon
Photograph by Stephen Stewart, Stephen Stewart Photographs, ONE Archives at the USC Libraries

p. 29 – Black Cat Protest
Advocate Records, ONE Archives at the USC Libraries

p. 30 – Frank Kameny
Photograph by Nancy Tucker, Nancy M. Tucker Philadelphia Reminder Day Photographs, ONE Archives at the USC Libraries

p. 31 – Reed Erickson
Reed L Erickson Papers, ONE Archives at the USC Libraries

p. 32 – Gene Compton's Cafeteria Riot Sign
Photograph by Gaylesf, Public Domain, https://commons.wikimedia.org/w/index.php?curid=2280164

p. 33 – Vanguard Journal Covers
ONE Archives Periodical Collection, ONE Archives at the USC Libraries

GAY LIBERATION

p. 34 – Chapter Image
Photograph by Pat Rocco, Pat Rocco Photographs and Papers, ONE Archives at the USC Libraries

p. 37 – Carolyn Weathers and Friends
Carolyn Weathers Photographs and Papers, ONE Archives at the USC Libraries

p. 40 – Jack Baker and Mike McConnell
Photograph by Kay Tobin Lahusen, Barbara Gittings and Kay Tobin Lahusen Gay History Papers and Photographs, New York Public Library

p. 41 – Troy Perry in Car
Christopher Street West Association Collection, ONE Archives at the USC Libraries

p. 42 – White House delegation
Official White House photograph, George Raya Papers, ONE Archives at the USC Libraries

p. 42 – Elaine Noble
ONE Subject File Photographs, ONE Archives at the USC Libraries

p. 43 – Activists at Police Station
Photograph by Pat Rocco, Pat Rocco Papers, ONE Archives at the USC Libraries

p. 43 – Melvin Boozer
ONE Subject File Photographs, ONE Archives at the USC Libraries

p. 44 – Democratic National Convention Gay and Lesbian Delegates
Photograph by Allen G. Shores, Allen G. Shores Photographs, ONE Archives at the USC Libraries

p. 44 – Ivy Bottini
Ivy Bottini Papers, ONE Archives at the USC Libraries

p. 45 – State Steamship Lines Protest
Committee for Homosexual Freedom Collection, ONE Archives at the USC Libraries

p. 46 – Barbara Gittings
Photograph by Stephen Stewart, Stephen Stewart Photographs, ONE Archives at the USC Libraries

p. 47 – Gay Sunshine Cover
Gay Sunshine Records, ONE Archives at the USC Libraries

p. 47 – Jeanne Córdova
Jeanne Córdova Papers and Photographs, ONE Archives at the USC Libraries

p. 48 – Audre Lorde
Photograph by Stephen Stewart, Stephen Stewart Photographs, ONE Archives at the USC Libraries

PRIDE IN DIVERSITY

p. 50 – Chapter Image
Photograph by Pat Rocco, Pat Rocco Photographs and Papers, ONE Archives at the USC Libraries

p. 53 – Canyon Sam
Courtesy of Canyon Sam

p. 58 – Senior Action in Gay Environment
Photograph by Pat Rocco, Pat Rocco Photographs and Papers, ONE Archives at the USC Libraries

Appendices

p. 59 – Troy Perry
Photograph by Stephen Stewart, Stephen Stewart Photographs, ONE Archives at the USC Libraries

p. 60 – Angela Douglas
Photograph by Pat Rocco, Pat Rocco Photographs and Papers, ONE Archives at the USC Libraries

p. 60 – Sylvia Rivera
Photograph by Mariette Pathy Allen, courtesy of Mariette Pathy Allen

p. 63 – Kate Millet and Zoe Budapest
Jeanne Córdova Papers and Photographs, ONE Archives at the USC Libraries

RESPONSE TO ADVERSITY

p. 64 – **Chapter Image**
Photograph by Pat Rocco, Pat Rocco Photographs and Papers, ONE Archives at the USC Libraries

p. 66 – Anita Bryant protesters
Photograph by Pat Rocco, Pat Rocco Photographs and Papers, ONE Archives at the USC Libraries

p. 66 – Harvey Milk
Photograph by Marie Ueda, Marie Ueda Collection, Gay, Lesbian, Bisexual, Transgender Historical Society

p. 67 – Candlelight protesters
Photograph by Crawford Barton, Crawford Barton Papers, Gay, Lesbian, Bisexual, Transgender Historical Society

p. 68 – Steve Endean
Photograph by Stephen Stewart, Stephen Stewart Photographs, ONE Archives at the USC Libraries

p. 69 – March on Washington
Photograph by Pat Rocco, Pat Rocco Photographs and Papers, ONE Archives at the USC Libraries

THE AIDS ERA

p. 70 – Chapter Image
Photograph by Chuck Stallard, ACT UP/Los Angeles Records, ONE Archives at the USC Libraries

p. 73 – Dr. Mark Katz
Courtesy of Dr. Mark Katz

p. 77 – Larry Kramer
Photograph by David Shankbone, https://www.flickr.com/photos/27865228@N06/4484901239

p. 78 – Movie studio protest
Gay and Lesbian Alliance Against Defamation (GLAAD) Records, ONE Archives at the USC Libraries

p. 79 – AIDS graph
Centers for Disease Control and Prevention, HIV Surveillance Report, http://www.cdc.gov/hiv/library/reports/surveillance/index.html

p. 79 – Urvashi Vaid
Photograph by Jurek Wajdowicz, urvashivaid.net

p. 80 – Virginia Apuzzo
Photograph by Stephen Stewart, Stephen Stewart Photographs, ONE Archives at the USC Libraries

p. 81 – Silence=Death
ACT UP/Los Angeles Records, ONE Archives at the USC Libraries

p. 82 – Sisters of Perpetual Indulgence
Photograph by Marie Ueda, Marie Ueda Collection, Gay, Lesbian, Bisexual, Transgender Historical Society

p. 83 – Marlon Riggs
Courtesy of Equality Forum, http://lgbthistorymonth.com/marlon-riggs?tab=multimedia

p. 84 – Roberta Achtenberg
California State University, https://web.archive.org/web/20180404073140/http://www.calstate.edu/BOT/bios/achtenberg.shtml

p. 85 – Free Sharon Kowalski
ONE Subject Files Collection (print), Carolyn Weathers Photographs and Papers (photo), ONE Archives at the USC Libraries

p. 86 – Lou Sullivan
: Photograph by Mariette Pathy Allen, Louis G. Sullivan Papers, courtesy of Gay, Lesbian, Bisexual, Transgender Historical Society and Mariette Pathy Allen

p. 87 – NAMES Project quilt
: Harold "Mac" McCarthy Photographs and Papers, ONE Archives at the USC Libraries

LGBT RIGHTS MOVEMENT

p. 90 – Chapter Image
: Gay Event Photographs, ONE Archives at the USC Libraries

p. 93 – Paul Katami and Jeff Zarrillo
: Courtesy of Paul Katami and Jeff Zarrillo

p. 94 – Virginia Uribe
: Courtesy of Virginia Uribe

p. 97 – Bias Breakdown Graph
: Federal Bureau of Investigation, Uniform Crime Reports, Hate Crime Statistics, http://www.fbi.gov/about-us/cjis/ucr/ucr-publications#Hate

p. 98 – Leonard Matlovich
: Photograph by David, https://www.flickr.com/photos/bootbearwdc/13203725/, https://creativecommons.org/licenses/by/2.0/

p. 101 – Marriages
: Edgar Sandifer Papers (bottom right); Philadelphia Gay Wedding Photographs (bottom left); Photograph by Pat Rocco, Pat Rocco Papers, (top right) ONE Archives at the USC Libraries. Cora Latz and Etta Perkins Photographs, Gay, Lesbian, Bisexual, Transgender Historical Society

p. 102 – Anthony Sullivan and Richard Adams
: Photograph by Stephen Stewart, Stephen Stewart Photographs, ONE Archives at the USC Libraries

p. 103 – White House
: White House Photographer (White House Press Office), public domain via Wikimedia Commons

p. 105 – Michael Saum
: Courtesy of Michael Saum

p. 109 – Andrea Jenkins
: Photograph by Tony Webster, https://commons.wikimedia.org/wiki/File:Andrea_Jenkins_-_Minneapolis_City_Council_Vice_President,_Ward_8_(38891113634)_(cropped).jpg

p. 109 – Kim Coco Iwamoto
: Photograph by Linda Ching, http://commons.wikimedia.org/wiki/File:Kim_Coco_Iwamoto.jpg

p. 110 – Transgender Hate Crimes
: Photo by Jenny Jigour, courtesy of Jenny Jigour (left); Photo by Mariette Pathy Allen, courtesy of Mariette Pathy Allen (right)

EPILOGUE

p. 112 – Cover Image
: LGBT Solidary Rally, Photograph by mathiaswasik from New York City, https://flickr.com/photos/76783588@N00/31901673123

p. 115 – Transgender Military Ban Protest
: By Ted Eytan from Washington, DC, https://www.flickr.com/photos/taedc/36262659735/

p. 115 – Black Lives Matters Founders
: Black Lives Matter, https://blacklivesmatter.com/herstory/; Marsha P. Johnson Instittue, https://marshap.org/staff-and-board/

p. 117 – Diversity in the Community
: (A/PLG) Christopher Street West Association Records; (We Are Family) Christopher Street West Association Collection; (Queer Yiddishists) Twice Blessed Collection; (five people) Photograph by Vaughn Taylor, Vaughn Taylor Photographs; (lesbian couple, Black Gays Unite, Latinos Unidos) Photographs by Pat Rocco, Pat Rocco Papers; (Sisters of Perpetual Indulgence) Photograph by William S. Tom, William S. Tom Photographs; (woman in wheelchair) Photograph by Chuck Stallard, ACT UP/Los Angeles Records; ONE Archives at the USC Libraries.

APPENDICES

p. 118 – Cover Image
: Photograph by Chuck Stallard, ACT UP/Los Angeles Records; ONE Archives at the USC Libraries.

BIBLIOGRAPHY

GENERAL HISTORIES

Bronski, Michael. *A Queer History of the United States.* Boston: Beacon Press, 2011.

Clendinen, Dudley and Adam Nagourney. *Out for Good: The Struggle to Build a Gay Rights Movement in America.* New York: Simon & Schuster, 1999.

D'Emilio, John. *Sexual Politics, Sexual Communities: the Making of a Homosexual Minority in the United States, 1940-1970.* Chicago: The University of Chicago Press, 1983.

Eaklor, Vicki L. *Queer America: A GLBT History of the 20th Century.* Westport, Connecticut: Greenwood Press, 2008.

Eisenbach, David. *Gay Power: An American Revolution.* New York: Carroll & Graf Publishers, 2006.

Faderman, Lilian. *The Gay Revolution: The Story of the Struggle.* New York: Simon & Schuster, 2015.

Hirshman, Linda. *Victory: The Triumphant Gay Revolution.* New York: Harper Perennial, 2012.

Loughery, John. *The Other Side of Silence: Men's Lives and Gay Identities: A Twentieth-Century History.* New York: Henry Holt and Company, Inc., 1998.

McGarry, Molly and Fred Wasserman. *Becoming Visible: An Illustrated History of Lesbian and Gay Life in Twentieth-Century America.* New York: New York Public Library and Penguin Studio, 1998.

Thompson, Mark (ed.). *Long Road to Freedom: The Advocate History of the Gay and Lesbian Movement.* New York: St. Martin's Press, 1994.

SPECIFIC TOPICS AND ERAS

Bullough, Vern L. *Before Stonewall: Activists for Gay and Lesbian Rights in Historical Context.* Binghamton, New York: Harrington Park Press, 2002.

Faderman, Lillian. *Odd Girls and Twilight Lovers: A History of Lesbian Life in Twentieth-Century America.* New York: Columbia University Press, 1991.

Johnson, David K. *The Lavender Scare: The Cold War Persecution of Gays and Lesbians in the Federal Government.* Chicago: The University of Chicago Press, 2004.

Loftin, Craig. *Letters to ONE: Gay and Lesbian Voices from the 1950s and 1960s.* Albany: State University of New York Press, 2012.

Loftin, Craig. *Masked Voices: Gay Men and Lesbians in Cold War America.* Albany: State University of New York Press, 2012.

Meyerowitz, Joanne. *How Sex Changed: A History of Transsexuality in the United States.* Cambridge: Harvard University Press, 2002.

Morrow, Deana F. and Laura Messinger, ed. *Sexual Orientation and Gender Expression in Social Work Practice: Working with Gay, Lesbian, Bisexual, and Transgender People.* New York: Columbia University Press, 2006.

Russo, Vito. *The Celluloid Closet: Homosexuality in the Movies.* Revised edition. New York: Harper and Row, Publishers, 1987.

Shilts, Randy. *And the Band Played on: Politics, People and the AIDS Epidemic.* New York: St. Martin's Press, 1987.

Shilts, Randy. *Conduct Unbecoming: Gays & Lesbians in the U.S. Military.* New York: St. Martins Press, 1993.

Streitmatter, Roger. *Unspeakable: The Rise of the Gay and Lesbian Press in America.* Boston: Faber and Faber, 1995.

Stryker, Susan. *Transgender History.* Berkeley: Seal Press, 2008.

LOCAL HISTORIES

Chauncey, George. *Gay New York: Gender, Urban Culture, and the Making of the Gay Male World.* New York: BasicBooks, 1994.

Faderman, Lillian and Stuart Timmons. *Gay L.A.: A History of Sexual Outlaws, Power Politics, and Lipstick Lesbians.* New York: BasicBooks, 2006.

Frantz, David, and Mia Locks, ed. *Cruising the Archive: Queer Art and Culture in Los Angeles, 1945-1980*. Los Angeles: ONE National Gay & Lesbian Archives, 2012.

Stryker, Susan and Jim Van Buskirk. *Gay by the Bay: A History of Queer Culture in the San Francisco Bay Area*. San Francisco: Chronicle Books, 1996.

LEGAL HISTORIES

Ball, Carlos A. *From the Closet to the Courtroom: Five LGBT Rights Lawsuits that have Changed our Nation*. Boston: Beacon Press, 2010.

Eskridge, William N., Jr. *Dishonorable Passions: Sodomy Laws in America, 1961-2003*. New York: Viking, 2008.

Eskridge, William N., Jr. *Gaylaw: Challenging the Apartheid of the Closet*. Boston: Harvard University Press, 2002.

Mezey, Susan Gluck. *Queers in Court: Gay Rights Law and Public Policy*. Lanham, Maryland: Bowman & Littlefield Publishers, Inc., 2007.

Murdoch, Joyce, and Deb Price. *Courting Justice: Gay Men and Lesbians v. the Supreme Court*. New York: Basic Books, 2001.

BIOGRAPHIES

Bronski, Michael, ed. *Outstanding Lives: Profiles of Lesbians and Gay Men*. Detroit: Visible Ink Press, 1997.

Koop, C. Everett. *Koop: The Memoirs of America's Family Doctor*. New York, NY: Random House, 1991.

Russell, Paul. *The Gay 100: A Ranking of the Most Influential Gay Men and Lesbians, Past and Present*. New York: A Citadel Press Book, 1995.

Queen of the Neighborhood. *Revolutionary Women: A Book of Stencils*. Oakland, California: PM Press, 2010.

Timmons, Stuart. *The Trouble with Harry Hay: Founder of the Modern Gay Movement*. Boston: Alyson Publications, 1990.

REFERENCE AND ESSAY BOOKS

Burles, Kenneth T., ed. *Gay, Lesbian, Bisexual, Transgender Events*. 2 vols. Pasadena, CA: Salem Press, 2007.

D'Emilio, John. *The World Turned: Essays on Gay History, Politics, and Culture*. Duke University Press, 2002.

D'Emilio, John, William B. Turner, and Urvashi Vaid. *Creating Change: Sexuality, Public Policy and Civil Rights*. New York: St. Martins Press, 2000.

Hawley, John, ed. *LGBTQ America Today: An Encyclopedia*. 3 vols. Westport, CT: Greenwood Press, 2009.

Kranz, Rachel, and Tim Cusick. *Gay Rights*. New York: Facts On File, Inc., 2000.

Smith, Raymond A., ed. *Encyclopedia of AIDS*. Chicago, IL: Fitzroy Dearborn, 1998.

Stein, Marc. *LGBT Encyclopedia of Lesbian, Gay, Bisexual, and Transgender History in America*. New York: Charles Scribner's Sons, 2004.

WEBSITES

Affirmation: Gay & Lesbian Mormons.
www.affirmation.org

American Civil Liberties Union.
www.aclu.org/lgbt-rights

The AIDS Memorial Quilt.
www.aidsquilt.org

Gay and Lesbian Victory Fund.
www.victoryfund.org

Gay, Lesbian & Straight Education Network.
www.glsen.org

GLAAD.
www.glaad.org

GLBTQ: An Encyclopedia of Gay, Lesbian, Bisexual, Transgender, & Queer Culture. (Summers, Claude J., ed.)
www.glbtq.com

Appendices

Human Rights Campaign.
www.hrc.org

International Transgender Day of Remembrance.
www.transgenderdor.org

Intersex Society of North America.
www.isna.org

It Gets Better Project.
www.itgetsbetter.org

Lambda Legal.
www.lambdalegal.org

Metropolitan Community Churches.
mccchurch.org

National Center for Transgender Equality.
transequality.org

National Gay & Lesbian Task Force.
www.thetaskforce.org

Point Foundation.
www.pointfoundation.org

Transgender Law Center.
transgenderlawcenter.org

The Trevor Project.
www.thetrevorproject.org

GOVERNMENT WEBSITES

Federal Bureau of Investigation. Uniform Crime Reports. Hate crime statistics.
http://www.fbi.gov/about-us/cjis/ucr/ucr-publications#Hate

Centers for Disease Control and Prevention. HIV Surveillance Report.
http://www.cdc.gov/hiv/library/reports/surveillance/index.html

Library of Congress. Lesbian, Gay, Bisexual and Transgender Pride Month.
http://www.loc.gov/lgbt

ARCHIVAL WEBSITES

Cornell University. 25 Years of Political Influence: The Records of the Human Rights Campaign.
http://rmc.library.cornell.edu/HRC/exhibition/stage/stage_19.html

Gay, Lesbian, Bisexual, Transgender Historical Society.
www.glbthistory.org

The June Mazer Archives.
http://www.mazerlesbianarchives.org

Lesbian Herstory Archives.
http://www.lesbianherstoryarchives.org

The Kinsey Institute.
http://www.kinseyinstitute.org/library/archives.html

New York Public Library. Gay and Lesbian Collections – AIDS/HIV Collections.
http://www.nypl.org/locations/tid/36/node/138008

ONE National Gay & Lesbian Archives at the University of Southern California Libraries.
https://www.onearchvies.org
https://one.usc.edu/

San Francisco Public Library. James C. Hormel Gay & Lesbian Center.
http://sfpl.org/index.php?pg=0200002401

University of Michigan. Research Guide: LGBTQ Archives.
http://guides.lib.umich.edu/content.php?pid=29017&sid=211789

The Transgender Archives at the University of Victoria.
http://transgenderarchives.uvic.ca

Yale University. Guide to Resources in Manuscripts and Archives on Sexuality and Gender.
http://guides.library.yale.edu/content.php?pid=20186&sid=152703.

Yale Research Initiative on the History of Sexualities.
http://yrihs.yale.edu/resources/rame-collection

WIKIPEDIA PAGES

Bisexuality in the United States

History of bisexuality

Intersex human rights

LGBT

LGBT movements in the United States

LGBT rights in the United States

LGBT social movements

History of transgender people in the United States

Transgender

Transgender rights in the United States

www.ingramcontent.com/pod-product-compliance
Lightning Source LLC
Chambersburg PA
CBHW050753110526
44592CB00003B/54